WILD NEPHIN

SEÁN LYSAGHT

WILD NEPHIN

Seán Lysght

Stonechat Editions

First published in 2020

Stonechat Editions
Fahy
Westport
County Mayo
Ireland
F28 YD65

ISBN 978-0-9568918-4-6

Typeset in Perpetua

Printed and bound by KPS Colour Print Ltd., Knock,
County Mayo

No description of a route in this book should be taken to
imply the existence of a public right of way or access.

To the memory of Maurice Harford (1931-2019)

Contents

WILD NEPHIN

Lahardaun

NEPHIN ◄

Bofeenaun

Crumpaun River

KNOCKAFERTAGH ◄

BIRREENCORRAGH ◄

Lough Dahybaun

Bunaveela Lough

BUCKOOGH ◄

River Deel

Sheeragh River

Bellacorick

Altnabrocky River

Srahmore River

NEPHIN BEG ◄

Glennamong River

Lough Furnace

Black Oak River

Newport

CORSLIEVE ◄

Owenmore

Brogaunnamraher River

ANGEL MT. ◄

Corry Lough

BEN GORM ◄

Lough Feeagh

Bangor

Tarsaghaunmore River

Owenduff

Bellaveeny River

GREENAUN MT. ◄

River

Owengarve

Mulranny

Ballycroy •

N

>200M

0   5km

An arctic traveller once asked an Eskimo man about happiness, about exhilaration, and he answered, 'To come across fresh bear tracks and be ahead of all the other sledges.'

Barry Lopez, *Arctic Dreams*

WILD NEPHIN

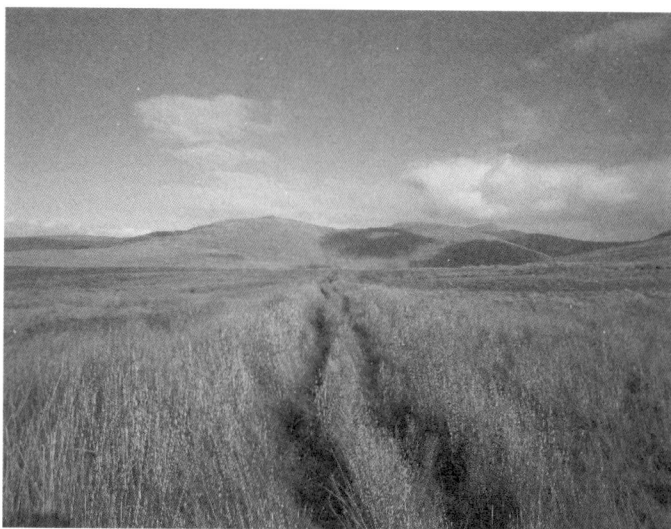

Introduction

I first saw Erris and the Nephin Beg Mountains in early April 1994 when my wife and I passed through the area on our way from Sligo to Westport. Our Easter road trip from Dublin to the north-west had been rattled for three days by freezing winds and spectacular hail showers, but there was a clearance on the fourth day as we drove from Bangor to Mulranny, with the snow-covered ridges of the mountains in the distance. Despite the winter asperities of that passing visit, we were stunned by the scale and remoteness of the region as its moorland and mountains glowed in the gentle light of a low sun just about to slip away.

Our retreat from Sligo to north-west Mayo was a kind of cultural shift too, from the heavy accretions of Yeats Country to an area that was very lightly inscribed, if at all, by writerly tradition. If I had caught echoes of Erris, it was only as a region of forbidding emptiness, mentioned by Robert Lloyd Praeger in *The Way that I Went* (1937) as 'almost frightening' in its loneliness. At the time, I was much preoccupied with Praeger's writings, including his monumental survey of Clare Island in Clew Bay, so that north-west Mayo for me was less a literary possession than a territory in the keeping of botanists, naturalists and topographers. A secular landscape untamed by the emotional harness of poetry – and no less interesting for that.

A few months later, a teaching job came up at the newly established Castlebar Campus of the Galway Regional Technical College, and by late September Jessica, my son Seamus and I had moved to Mayo on a western adventure. Given the demands of the move and a career teaching a newly minted discipline called Heritage, it was a few years before I started to explore north Mayo properly.

One day in mid-July, armed with the OS sheet for the area, my friend Michael Kingdon and I climbed Corslieve at the northern end of the Nephin Beg Range. We walked in from the west, through the valley of the Tarsaghaunmore River, a tributary of the Owenduff, and climbed the flank of the mountain onto the long ridge that rises from Maumykelly to the summit at 721 metres. Our interests that day were mostly natural, not historical. My notes from that excursion make no mention of the great cairn at the summit associated with the giant Dáithí Bán. Instead, we were fascinated to see salmon moving in a remote pool; I counted common sandpiper territories along the stony margins of the river and kept a record of grouse on the heathery slopes, and wheatears on rocky terrain close to the summit. Our energy and enthusiasm took us all the way down to Lough Nambracceagh on the far side of the mountain, where we fished for dark little mountain trout. We then tramped back through the pass at Maumykelly (Mám Uí Cheallaigh, Kelly's Pass) and returned across the open valley at the top of the Tarsaghaunmore catchment.

Nine days later, Michael and I walked into the same area, this time approaching along the larger Owenduff, a spate river that drains the entire western flank of the Nephin Beg Mountains. To use angling parlance, the river was working well after heavy rain overnight. Again, we had our fly rods, and they guided us like antennae across the bog, towards the waterfall at Scardaun (scairdeán, a cascade); rain and cloud had closed in as we toiled up the slope towards the lakes on the saddle between Corslieve and Nephin Beg. A flock of dunlin and ringed plover took off in the mist, the plover calling with that plaintive note which is familiar from the seashore, but which now seemed attuned to the desolation of the mountain.

We had a good afternoon's sport with the small mountain trout, and by the time we had finished, the weather had cleared. As we got back to the top of the cascade, a glorious view of the Owenduff catchment had opened up, in perfect evening stillness, the locháns of the flow like pieces of mirror set in the brown velvet of the bog. Achill was reduced to an angular abstraction of smoky blue, Paul-Henry style. In the windless calm of that evening, the threat of midges kept us going through the long kilometres back to the track; it was almost dark as we stepped carefully across the oily sheen of the river.

These were my first forays into a territory that was rarely visited: at the Scardaun lakes a few bits of litter, a pair of rusty scissors and a broken float were signs of fishermen; the Bangor Trail walking route, which runs through the area, was virtually unmarked by boot prints. The bog road into the upper Owenduff came to an end at a fishery cottage, with another abandoned house nearby filled with bales of shorn fleece. Out on the open bog, only the remains of a few stone cottages and field systems were signposts to an older time.

But at Tarsaghaun, three houses were still occupied, forming what locals referred to as 'the village', translating the Irish word 'baile' for any small cluster of settlement. Paddy McHugh was still alive then, living in the middle cottage with his son Paud. As I came back on other visits, I used to park at Paddy's, and would often be invited into his house for tea and a chat. Like most men from that part of Mayo, he had spent many years in England, involved in the post-war building boom – but Paddy was also a figure from a much older world.

There was a giant, Dáille Bhán, on the top of Corslieve one time, he told me. He lived at Leachta – the summit cairn – and 'he's buried outside Corick in a lake on the left as you go to Ballina.' Dáithí Bán's coffin at the bottom of the lake was twenty-four feet long. He reported this as the most striking thing about the area, an actual fact. There used to be another giant on Claggan Mountain, and a third at Castlehill, near Ballycroy. Paddy's account of the most famous giant of Erris was corroborated by other records in the published folklore. Dáithí Bán had given his name to Lough Dahybaun outside Bellacorick, where he reputedly died having been pursued there by an obscure band of monks. I later discovered that the third giant at Castlehill was associated with a fine megalithic wedge tomb visible from the main road.

I am grateful to have known Paddy McHugh for a couple of years before ill health took him away from his cottage at Tarsaghaun. He died in 2006 at the age of ninety and is buried in the windswept cemetery at Fahy, close to the sea. His father, he once told me, came from Achill, and spoke Irish to his children, but emigration, especially, compelled a shift from Irish to English: 'all Ballycroy has gone over to English now,' he said. This linguistic and cultural shift took place all over north Mayo in the twentieth century, to a point where Irish barely survives as a vernacular in the extreme north-west and on the Mullet Peninsula.

The folklorists and linguists of the Irish Folklore Society and the Government's Folklore Commission were well aware of these changes, in Mayo and elsewhere, and so they devoted a considerable effort to recording the older culture before it disappeared. Articles in *Béaloideas*, the Folklore Society's journal, contain stories, superstitions, riddles and historical lore from native speakers across the Wild Nephin area, from Bellacorick in the east to Mulranny and Tieranaur in the west. In the 1920s, 30s and 40s, there were still native speakers left, including a few storytellers, *seanchaithe* with richly stored memories. But by then, there was a sense that Irish was facing extinction in the region; the situation is dramatised in an encounter in 1920 between one of the collectors, Michael Mac Henry, and Seán Mac Manamon of Bellacorick. When Mac Henry first caught up with Mac Manamon just outside Bangor Erris and addressed him in Irish, 'you would think that I had come down to him from heaven, such was the welcome he gave me,' he later wrote.[1]

The work of these folklorists has preserved a lot of historical memory of the area in print and digital archives, despite the sad decline of the Irish vernacular. (And there is a great wealth of Mayo material still in unpublished notebooks in UCD's folklore archive.)[2] If the great tide of Irish has drained away from Wild Nephin, fragments of that speech still survive in its placenames. Paddy McHugh had some residual memory of Irish, allowing him to translate some of them: 'Casadh na Leice', he explained, was a big pool in the river with an overhanging rock where the river turned; 'Pollín Breac' was a shallow stretch just upstream from his house, a good spot for sea trout. Other placenames in Paddy's repertoire were corrupted despite retaining their native phonetic flavour: Éadan ó Thuaidh, the northern brow, had become Éadan Dhubha; Tamhnach na Sifín, the field of the corn stalks, had been modified into Tamlesheffaun. Without the guidance of a living language, Irish placenames have a tendency to become detached from their origins and take on a purely phonetic existence in the mouths of local people. Restoring them to their proper meaning involves solving a whole series of fascinating cruxes, as Tim Robinson has done as a writer and mapmaker in his work on Galway and north Clare. Some of the same archaeology of language has been applied to Mayo by Séamas Ó Catháin, Uinsionn Mac Craith, the late Fiachra MacGabhann, Barry Dalby, and others; there is now a precious web of meanings cast by these names over the bogs, rivers and mountains, woven by researchers from surviving threads of knowledge. And still, there are many puzzles of origin to mull over and consider, whose solution was probably snatched away by the winds of the twentieth century when a whole generation left Mayo to look for work and opportunity in post-war Britain.

The name Nephin, from Irish Néifinn, is itself a rich set of suggestions and associations, taking us all the way back to pre-Christian antiquity. It broadly means a sacred place or a sanctuary, and was used in this way in early Irish, and in an associated early Christian sense to mean a small chapel or oratory. Beyond this tradition of reference, we glimpse an older Celtic element, which directs us to Nemetona, a goddess of the sacred grove, revered in ancient Gaul, whose cult is recorded from Bath in Roman times. This pre-Christian ancestry for Nephin gains considerable weight from older references to north-west Mayo as Irrus Domnann, Erris of the Dumnonii, an early Celtic people whose territorial name survives in England as Devon. The English writer Roger Deakin has traced many examples of placenames in the old Devon territory of the Dumnonii with the element Nymet, Nymph and Nympton, all referring to local rivers, with a common etymology in Gaulish *nemeton*. In Deakin's chapter, 'The Sacred Groves of Devon', in his 2007 masterpiece *Wildwood*, he directs us to an ancient pre-Christian landscape of sacred woods and rivers, not to mountaintops; therefore in our imaginative excursion into pre-Christian north Mayo, while the mighty cone of Nephin might be the signpost to a tuath or tribal territory, it was not the mountaintop itself, but the lowland groves and rivers that were zones of sanctity. This idea is reinforced by the apparent absence of any ancient ritual practice on Nephin, or of any association with the pre-Christian cult of Crom Dubh (Black Stoop), whose Lughnasa festival is widely recorded at other summits in the country.

Many of these antiquarian speculations take place nowadays in a thinly populated outdoor space; the bogs and uplands are not populated as they used to be, and it is rare to meet casually anyone out on the hills who could verify or locate a toponym. Instead, a new identity has been given to the area with the creation of the Ballycroy Wild Nephin National Park, and the designation of a large forest wilderness to the east in the townlands of Letterkeen, Gaulaun, Tawnynanulty, and Altnabrocky. Over 15,000 hectares, with the Corslieve massif at its core, are now dedicated to what one of the planning documents calls 'primitive recreation' and the direct encounter between the visitor and the landscape. The watchwords for this new promotional definition are the highly contested ideas of 'wild', 'wilderness', and 'rewilding'; and in the process, Wild Nephin is drawn into a kind of crossfire of debate about how this wilderness should be managed. In an era bristling with official designations and policies about tourism, rural development and conservation, the north Mayo wilderness is now inhabited by a new language governing woodland and peatland restoration, carbon sequestration, light pollution, habitat management, salmonid conservation, tourism infrastructure, visitor impact, and so on. You could add the elephant in the room

– namely, grazing pressures as a result of high sheep numbers across much of the district.

Whether the wild and wilderness can ever be the outcome of official intervention is a moot point, even where trees are being lovingly planted in parts of the Nephins by the National Parks and Wildlife Service as part of their rewilding project. An older, and still serviceable idea of wildness sees it as the outcome of neglect, where things 'run' or 'go' wild when the husbandry of gardening and agriculture is withdrawn, as happened in the exclusion zone around Chernobyl. Many fascinating corners of this landscape fall outside designated reserves and conservation areas: rocky gorges cut by the action of streams over centuries where ferns and mosses thrive; old farmyards choked with brambles, ash and willow where thrushes and other birds find nesting places; a derelict building by a river where grey wagtails breed in an overgrown wall; peacock butterflies on buddleia in a disused industrial yard. Nature can thrive in corners like these just as happily as in designated places, evading our definitions, surprising us with her resilience, like the blackcaps that sing in Castlebar around the Castle Street car park in the old convent grounds. One of the keenest witnesses to this facet of nature, the Shropshire writer Paul Evans, declared recently that 'the more I look, the more I find the wild everywhere, hiding in plain sight.'[3]

In any case, ideas of the wild and rewilding are contested these days and come with an apparatus of disagreement: should coniferous forests in protected areas be removed or allowed to 'grow on' and form a new kind of woodland? How many foxes and corvids should be killed to help ground-nesting birds? What are sustainable numbers of red deer in Wild Nephin? Which raptor species should be prioritised for a reintroduction programme: osprey, sea eagle or goshawk? Debates like these are probably an outcome of many people's attachment to wilderness – however questionable that idea might be. The wild can be anything from a corporate exercise in tourist promotion to a deep-seated nostalgia for Edenic origins. Wherever it sits on the scale of our interests and imaginings, it has a new frontier in north Mayo with the Wild Nephin Wilderness Area and National Park, a future-oriented project with an ambitious timescale: the National Parks and Wildlife Service has leased land from Coillte for fifty years, and is planning a restoration process that will outlive many of its current promoters.

These developments were still at the planning stage when I started my wanderings almost twenty years ago with fishing rod, binoculars and rucksack. Tarsaghaunmore was the heartland of that wilderness from the outset, and that broad, shallow valley with its meandering stream under the western flank of Corslieve remains for me a land of the heart where half-remembered remnants of an older culture still mark an open space with slight graduations: an old livestock enclosure, ruined levees, a few stone cottages, the traces of booley shelters. There is an intensity here that is different from pure desertion: the records suggest that people knew this terrain as part of their lives, moving here for the summer pasture, taking the trail along the river to bring milk and butter back to the coastal village, hunting salmon in the holding pools between April and September, and then returning in winter to hunt geese and red grouse. My visits are a kind of reverence and awe at the resilience of those people who could be at home in a landscape that offers very few comforts, and which attracted few settlers in ancient times: the antiquarian map of the Nephin Beg area is largely blank once you move away from the coast.

My knowledge was later extended when I started exploring the Owenduff catchment farther south, as an angler and casual walker. The Owenduff catchment has all the remoteness and exposure of Tarsaghaunmore, although on a larger scale, and its important salmon river is more actively watched by fisheries officers and keepers. One of the Owenduff's credentials as a wild river is that forestry has encroached only slightly on the catchment, and is absent from its upper stretches, so the landscape of open blanket bog is largely intact and nothing obtrudes between the visitor and the wide horizon of mountain stretching from Maumykelly and Corslieve in the north, to Claggan Mountain at the southern end near Mulranny.

This thirty-kilometre curving line of mountains holds much of Erris in its cradle, an open vista of mountain, bog, estuary and shore where land gives way to water undramatically, in an obscure series of beaches, mudflats and tidal creeks. Erris (Iorras in Irish) means peninsula, but the western fringe of the barony comprises not one but many peninsulas, many of which are invisible from the main N59 on its way from Mulranny to Belmullet via Bangor. The road is a compromise shunning the barrier of mountains to the east, and the low-lying, soft indentations of coast to the west. In 'The Peninsula', a poem perfectly attuned to the experience of driving this stretch of road, Seamus Heaney wrote, 'The sky is tall as over a runway,/The land without marks so you will not arrive//But pass through, though always skirting landfall.' Nor does this western edge have any of the wild drama you would expect from the sea: the main swell of the Atlantic slams against the ramparts of Achill Island and the Mullet

Peninsula, spending its force, and arrives as a diminished pulse of waves lapping against the muds, sands and gravels of the Erris margin.

Whereas this western coastal fringe defies the usual standard of dramatic scenery with its unbroken distances, the terrain is different once you get into the mountains and discover the territory to the east. Some of this is owing to the impact of glaciation, especially marked on the lee of the Corslieve massif, where snow lying on the sheltered eastern side built up into glaciers, scouring out a magnificent series of corries. The same glacial action produced a dramatic arête along the rim of Glendahurk (Gleann Dá Thorc, the valley of two peaks) dividing the Owenduff catchment to the north from Clew Bay to the south. The corries and moraines of this glaciated country have many lonely lakes or tarns shimmering at the base of imposing cliffs; in high summer these theatres of light, water and rock often echo with the scolding calls of nesting ravens and peregrines. The views to the east towards Lough Conn and north towards the wind turbines at Bellacorick have their own imposing scale, rivalling the vistas in the west; but modern coniferous plantations have transformed the spaces immediately to the east of the Nephin Beg Mountains. The Irish state carried out some of its earliest forestry plantings in the flow country here, smothering a rich habitat in dense stands of lodgepole pine, sitka spruce and Japanese larch. A large area of this forestry, now referred to as the Nephin Forest, is managed by NPWS alongside the National Park, ensuring that veteran trees from the 1950s and 60s are now growing on as part of a new woodland legacy. Wind blow and poor ground conditions have depleted many of the original stands, but natural processes are taking over, and some broadleaves, heathers and other plants are returning with the incursion of light. With all these influences, and ambitious management plans, the Nephin Forest is an evolving and unprecedented environment.

Some of my explorations were given focus and purpose several years ago when I set out to visit places in Mayo where eagles had been reported in the nineteenth and twentieth centuries prior to their extinction around the time of the First World War. This was a summer programme of walks to several peaks in the area, and extended beyond Wild Nephin to other parts of the country. My account of that year's discoveries was published by Little Toller Books as *Eagle Country* (2018), and the positive response to the book encouraged me to continue my journey. This time I set out to explore the winter season as a counterpart to the summer described in *Eagle Country*.

The following chapters are a kind of extended journal of those walks, from October to March, in different areas of Wild Nephin. I knew that winter seemed to lack many of the advantages of summer, in the absence of most flowering plants and breeding birds, and with constraints of weather and day-length. But the desertion and – at times – desolation suited my temperament; winter would allow me to put my own attention and Wild Nephin itself to a test: as Thoreau said about his experiment with life at Waldon Pond in Massachusetts: 'I wanted… to reduce it to its lowest terms.' Winter suggested itself as a new perspective of this kind, something akin to what Heaney referred to in 'The Peninsula' as 'Water and ground in their extremity.'

So I set out with Barry Dalby's recently produced map to experience winter days in Wild Nephin, in a few instances revisiting sites I had covered on my earlier eagle trail but mostly venturing into new places, and gradually extending my coverage. There was a primitive satisfaction in expanding my territory verbally, in building up a prose map of the landscape; at the same time, I felt free of the need to be strictly systematic, so I followed distractions and whims as they arose.

WEST

A Walk to Eagle Crag

In Erris in early October there's a sharpening of light as the sun declines to a lower angle and throws longer shadows across the road during the day: the air is getting ready for the first frosts; leaf margins are going orange and brown; purple moor grass (*Molinia*) is turning a rust colour which will transform entire landscapes over the next few weeks.

As I drive north past Ballycroy, a brisk wind is tousling the vegetation along the road, adding to a giddiness, a disorientation amounting almost to unease in the unfathomable space of Erris's great expanse. My attention is caught by fresh stacks of pine logs in a clear-felled plantation: I pull off the road, walk two hundred yards of forestry track to take photographs of a twelve-foot-high wall of orange log sections lining the track and to breathe in the smell of fresh pine resin. Another gift to autumn's sharpened senses.

I cannot linger over these novelties – new clearances, freshly laid tracks – for long, because the shorter days impose time constraints on the walker. I drive on and turn off the main road a few kilometres after Ballycroy towards the settlement at Tarsaghaun. A pair of proud Mayo county flags have been tied to road signs at either side of the entrance; these are now fully extended by the wind, as if the elements themselves were underlining allegiance and identity.

The tarred track into Tarsaghaun runs in a straight line across blanket bog, with a partially felled forestry plantation to the left. The first stretch rises gently to a brae or elevation which blocks the view of the houses beyond, so that at first sight this might be a road to nowhere, losing itself in the undulations of moorland. After a kilometre or so, the settlement comes into view: a group of three occupied houses and fields spread on either side of the eponymous river, the Tarsaghaunmore.

The scarred and patched track, with its parallel sequence of electricity poles and cables, is a modern intrusion into this landscape: before the Irish Free State brought its modernising influence, the way into and out of Tarsaghaun was a stony track following the river. This led downstream to the junction with the larger Owenduff, not far from its estuary on Blacksod Bay, where fresh water spreads out into the vast sandy flats at Croy. In the old days, the journey to Tarsaghaun was on foot, perhaps accompanied by a donkey or pony.

As I park at McHugh's cottage, my arrival provokes a border collie to bark and rattle the chain he is secured by. His owner, Paud, old Paddy's son, usually appears to greet me, but today there is no sign of him. With Paud absent this morning, I think my solitude is unbroken, but as I leave the car to set out, a man approaches on a quad bike and greets me. He is another local, his features weathered and worn like those of a desert tribesman. A spade and a stick are strapped across the frame at the front of his quad like ritual objects. On all my previous visits I have never met this man, but I chat with him respectfully as if I had finally been granted an audience with a king.

'It's windy today,' he says, raising his voice to make sure his message isn't dispersed by the stiff breeze buffeting his hood. I counter this challenge by saying, 'Yes, but it's mild,' a remark he has to agree with as I stake my claim to a place in the day. Once I tell him where I am from, and where I am going, he seems satisfied and we part company. He goes to call on another house, which I pass on my way out of the village.

My mission today is to view a cliff called Screigiolra, or Eagle Crag, on the side of a hill called Maumykelly, at the northern end of the Nephin Beg Range. Maumykelly is one of a series of smooth undulations and ridges that comprise the horizons ahead of me. Each ridge is a subtle variation on grey-brown, darkening with distance, unless the sun hits the scree falls of Corslieve, turning the flanks of the mountain silver. Despite the recent acquisition by the State of much of this ground to create the Wild Nephin National Park, this is still sheep country, with surviving Gaelic placenames that mark the traditional knowledge of the sheepmen in this forbidding terrain. There is also a diminishing stock of folklore and legend from a time when people walked these bogs and uplands as part of their daily lives.

I reach a high point on the track above the village and get my first view of the upper Tarsaghaun, a wide, shallow valley between gently contoured ridges. A glittering avenue of water runs along a grassy valley floor, where people built levees many generations ago to keep floodwater out of meadows, pastures and tillage. I lean into the wind and move on, marching smartly across the grassy levels – a place known locally as a srah (Ir. sraith), wherever sand and gravel deposits from flooding create drainage for grassland. Away to my left, there's one plantation of lodgepole pines swaying and hissing in the wind, as if in protest at empty space. But this will be the last intrusion of trees on my journey.

After that long srah, with its fencing to mark boundaries of ownership, are the roofless remains of a herder's stone cottage; a little farther on, a new footbridge takes walkers on the Bangor Trail across the river. This area seems consecrate to boundaries, exclusions and the transgressions that they imply; the place itself, Tairseachán Mór, translates as great threshold. Having negotiated my way past dogs, a king, and two gateways, I am at last free to cross and recross a river: in the absence of borders, the recent spate having receded, I can easily cross the shallow sections in wellingtons.

A kestrel is hovering over a hillside nearby, being drawn upwards like a yo-yo in the brisk wind. My attention shifts to the need to purify the simple act of walking by stripping it of the impulse to look, enquire, identify, and to concentrate instead on a series of decisions: when to cross the river to avoid the higher, peaty banks and follow the grassy levels; when to follow the meandering stream and when to cut out the loops by taking a straight line. If I could lose myself in these judgements, time and distance would pass more quickly, and I could conquer my impatience. I make these calculations because Maumykelly is still a long way off; although I have walked most of this valley before, the upper stretch of the catchment to the north is unknown to me.

At about midday, I reach the large pool in the river known as Casadh na Leice, the turn at the rocks. Here the river forms a deep, slow-moving pool; the southern bank is a twenty-foot slope ending in exposed bedrock just above the water. As I sit and eat a snack from my rucksack I think about all the salmon that have been killed here, illegally and legally, by net and rod, over the generations. The Tarsaghaunmore is a prolific river for salmon and sea trout; the angling rights are held by a well-off professional family from Dublin, and this ownership is still shadowed by an older tradition of poaching.

Nothing is showing today in the peaty water, just an angry jabble driven by gusts across the tail of the pool. When I check the time on my phone, I notice that I am out of coverage, so there's a sense that I am drifting gradually into the embrace of the lonely ridges rising from here to the top of Corslieve. Then, just as I get onto my feet to move on, a charm of seven goldfinches flies across the heathery bank above Casadh na Leice, announcing a life that is here, independent of phone networks and human traffic.

There's a difficult section of bog to cross close to Casadh na Leice: the uneven surface was explained to me as the result of people digging out old bog timber from the peat: some of the roots and stumps can still be seen sticking out at odd angles from eroding sections of riverbank, or dumped clear of the river by floodwater. After this, the river makes a wide S-shaped curve, and as I look ahead, I see a herd of cattle, like an apparition out of ancient times: it was the grassy places shaped by river depositions that first brought people and their livestock into these remote valleys from settlements near the coast. This pastoral tradition still endures within the National Park. Not far upstream from here are the fallen remains of an old stone enclosure or bawn (Ir. bábhún) that must have been built as a handling pen for sheep and cattle.

The river divides at this point into two higher catchments. One of these drains the dark, narrow glen of Díogan Mór, or great trench, which nestles close to the flank of the main mountain. I head left to follow the other catchment towards Maumykelly. Whereas the previous flood plain was the size of a football pitch, it is now only as wide as a tennis court. How far do the salmon run, I wonder, on their way upriver to spawn? Several years ago, I followed this river briefly before turning right to cross the bog on our way to Corslieve. It was July, the river level was low, and I was thrilled to see salmon moving in one of the pools.

The tributary, a kind of miniature Tarsaghaunmore, is much longer than I realised, with its own meanders, streams and pools; some of the best stretches are slow and deep, including one eighty-metre blade of mystery shining and wavering in its own trench. I probe the dark water with my stick to a depth of four or five feet. There's plenty of water here for spawning salmon.

The land along the main river is marked by levees and ridges of old field systems, but there are no marks of enclosure and cultivation here. I have only a few mountain sheep for company: they skitter away nervously when they see me, as if my purpose were to round up stragglers from the great flocks, numbering thousands, that were gathered in from these hills in a great drive just a couple of weeks ago. Late September is the time for rounding-up, involving a day-long, heroic, communal effort by the sheepmen and their dogs.

Eventually I tire of following the river and walk to the top of a bluff to get a better view of the ground ahead. The geography of this meandering river is finally fading away, diminishing into the sandy colour of blanket bog, with a bright skyscape of running clouds and transatlantic planes. Owing to an effect of perspective, the planes appear to be shifting at the same pace as the clouds, like a single image. One flock of about a dozen sheep is moving serenely across the bog, like a migrating herd, too far away to be disturbed by me. The sound of water chuckling over stones screens us from each other's hearing. I sit to eat a sandwich, drink water, check time and distance. I have over two kilometres to travel. Maumykelly is still a modest-looking spur off the mountain keeping its eagle crag away out of sight.

The only man-made feature in the landscape is in the distance, a stripe of forestry running along the base of a hill (the top of the hill is bare, like a monk's tonsure). The end of that plantation forms a point to the right of the hill, just opposite Screigiolra. The river divides here into a cluster of little streams, which are no more than dark lines forming seams in the bog: the local word for them is fiodán. The longest of these, Fiodán a' Mhám, the stream at the pass, runs all the way to Screigiolra, and it would be my guide route back home if the weather were to change. For now, though, walking conditions are excellent, and I strike out in a straight line across the wet bog at a place called Scrathán, a light green sward.

There was a night's rain thirty-six hours ago, so the ground is splashy in places, if firm underfoot. I rely on faint tracks made by sheep to steer me as economically as possible across these flats, though sometimes they transect my line at ninety degrees and I ignore them; at other times the trail fades out and my steps are unguided, until a faint line reasserts itself in the heather and I walk again in the animals' footsteps. The deep, gloomy valley of Díogan Mór has shifted away behind me now as I make progress into an unknown area. Another kestrel appears, then a raven, and a dragonfly; they serve only to underline the overwhelming fact of space and distance. There's still no view of Screigiolra, so I am turned in on my own hopes and motivation.

Now the scale of this landscape threatens to defeat me; I struggle with fatigue and a sense of frustration. The wet bog gives way to a drier area, where the heather is knee-deep rather than ankle-high. Then, as if to underline the quality of this habitat, a pair of red grouse explode from the ground next to me and fly away across the fiodán, uttering their throaty calls.

Red grouse are a headline species for conservation in the National Park, along with merlin, golden plover and white-fronted geese, and it was concern for these birds' future that spurred the EU to lock horns with the Irish government some years ago over its failure to curb overgrazing by sheep in the Mayo and Galway uplands. A major destocking programme followed, with the result that heather is recovering, providing food and shelter for moorland birds and other animals, and healing the dismal wasting that used to mark the Nephin Beg Mountains. This restored vegetation becomes an impediment as I flounder through tussocks of growth for the last hour.

I am spitting like a football player from the exertion, and I begin to curse the terrain. This is where you can understand the dour, quarrelsome temper of porters on expeditions overseas as they served colonial adventures. I'm detached from my own purpose now as I swear at the bitch of a ground. And then, my feeling alters, and I think of the Tudor and Cromwellian conquerors as they toiled through hostile wastes in Ireland, and how their contempt for the wilderness extended to the inhabitants themselves, and impelled their cruelty. But no one lives here now; my disorientation is my own, it belongs only to me.

The edge of the spur is finally looming ahead, along with the tapering point of the plantation on the far side, as I enter the saddle of the pass. Wind is being funnelled here between higher slopes, so the easterly picks up as I come round the spur, forcing me to look down towards calmer ground near the fiodán. The escarpment of Screigiolra comes into view: a steep portion of the flank of Maumykelly with a few outcropping rocks which barely amount to a cliff. For a moment I am not sure that I have arrived, but a check in my map confirms this as the old eagle breeding haunt I have come to see. This is a meagre site when compared to the towering cliff walls in the larger corries of the west, but the slopes here are gentler, the action of glaciation is not so pronounced, and the breeding eagles had fewer options.

I keep going to get closer to the crag: it is in fact the last and most pronounced in a series of six or seven ridges that emerge in relief from the hillside, like ribs. The first in the series are like giant versions of cultivation ridges, fit for a garden tended by Dáithí Bán, while the last two rise as exposed rocky crags: only the last in the series, Screigiolra, is steep or high enough to give shelter to an eagle's nest. A broad shoulder at the top of the crag is densely covered in tall heather, out of reach of grazing sheep. A single rowan tree, already denuded of its leaves, grows at the foot of the cliff, its branches raised towards the rock, like a priest worshipping at an altar. I estimate that the rocky face and the exposed shoulder are barely thirty feet high.

After I have taken photographs of this unusual series of ridges I take a last look at Screigiolra and notice that a few sheep have moved into position above the heathery shoulder, as if to declare their ownership of this place in the eagles' absence. Indeed, it is a long time since there were eagles here to catch the attention of travellers at the pass. The last golden eagle recorded in this area was a juvenile shot at Bangor Erris in October 1915; the specimen spent many years at Belvedere College in Dublin before being transferred to Glenveagh National Park in Donegal where it now forms part of the displays at the visitors' centre. I am tantalised by the thought that this unfortunate bird, one of the last in north Mayo, was reared on an eyrie at this site.

Shortly after I have turned back, retracing my steps, I realise that I am no longer under any time pressure: it is not

yet four o'clock, so I find a place to sit on the slope of the
spur with a superb view of the valley. I eat the rest of my
sandwich like a famished peasant and take a few swigs of the
Chardonnay-coloured water I took from the fiodán.
Suddenly, an agitation on a lower slope to my left catches
my eye: when I snatch the binoculars I discover a hen
harrier female in a mid-air kerfuffle with a small dark falcon
– a merlin. They tussle for a few moments just above the
ground, and then the larger bird floats away, showing
clearly the bright, white band at the base of its tail. The
wings are held in a wide, shallow V, like a child's glider; the
flight is rocking and buoyant as the skydancer fades away in
the distance and alights on the ground, now barely a speck,
over a kilometre away.

The valley has suddenly come alive: I see another bird, a
kestrel, hovering to my right, quartering the heathery levels
for small mammals, and when I fix it with the binoculars,
there's another distant speck in the sky, which turns out to
be a second kestrel hovering on its ledge of air. Three
raptor species in an instant; now all I need is a peregrine to
complete the moorland set.

The hen harrier is most unexpected: they do not breed in
Mayo, but the National Park rangers see them occasionally
in winter. It is over ten years since I last saw one in the
county. In England, the hen harrier is perhaps the most
politicised bird of all, on the verge of extinction as a
breeding species because of illegal killing on grouse moors.
Two hen harriers were shot on the Sandringham Estate in
Norfolk in 2007, an incident which put Prince Harry and
his friend William van Cutsem in the frame, although no
charges were ever brought. Six years later, my wife and I
were in Italy, at the Venice Biennale, and were amazed by
the picture of a huge hen harrier, also a female, with a

Range Rover in its talons, which dominated the entrance hall of the English pavilion. The picture was part of a multi-media show by Jeremy Deller, and made this bird an icon of protest against the arrogance of aristocratic landowners and their shooting clients. There have recently been calls for the licensing of shooting estates in an attempt to stop persecution. Ireland has its hen harrier politics too, because the species is vulnerable to wind-farm developments in the south-west, and it has been the subject of planning controversies relating to wind farms.

Just as the wilderness reaches its apotheosis in the hen harrier's appearance, I am aware of this species' legacy, of class divisions in the English landscape, of planning decisions in the Cork Kerry uplands. Even the vegetation here, a thriving, deepening carpet of ling, is the result of pressure from policymakers in Brussels and campaigners in Ireland to make the government honour its obligations under the EU Birds Directive. Where in all of this is wilderness to be found?

With a little time on my side, I can continue to sit for a while and think of my position in this remote place. I am almost absolved of the need to check maps and clocks because there is no danger of losing my way now or of running out of time. My fatigue has been dispersed by the wonder of an encounter between a hen harrier and a merlin, and of a sky animated by two hunting falcons. For a while, with my hunger sated, I can just *be*. Given a small measure of planning and experience, it is possible for a solitary walker to feel accommodated within a landscape such as this, and for this accommodation to amount to a belonging.

This is different from referring to such trips as excursions. In its root sense, excursion means to run out, or escape from bounds, into a place where we do not really belong, such as a wild landscape. Any benefits we draw from that will be enjoyed when we go back to our original setting, in the comfort of our homes. An excursion is an escape, and it expresses our strangeness when we reach a place where nature surrounds us.

I am dissatisfied with the idea of an excursion, of my day as an escape. Instead, there is a greater possibility: understanding the natural place as one where I belong – where we belong. That belonging is certainly different from the lives of the people who struggled for a meagre existence on the great expanse of Erris in earlier times, but it still amounts to *a way of being here*.

On my way back down the catchment, with the sun quite low in the western sky, the wind has fallen, and I can see fish stirring the quiet surface of the larger pools. There's not much else to attract my attention as I use my energies to follow the most economical trail back to the car. My thrifty steps get me there in three hours. The main distraction is the pyramid peak of Slievemore on Achill Island set in an amber sky in front of me, with the low promontory of Saddle Head just beyond. To get to Saddle Head, tucked away behind the mountains on the north-western tip of Achill, would be another day's walk, another strenuous exercise in belonging.

Back to Tarsaghaunmore

The spaces of Tarsaghaunmore, along with the neighbouring Owenduff catchment, have their own character of wildness, distance and desertion. They may be confined by Corslieve and the sickle of the Nephin Beg Mountains, but these open catchments impose their own terms of distance as you enter them; your human pace of progress gets reduced by the terrain, and the mountains are very slow to shift in the long perspective of those wide river valleys. At the same time, as you walk in, and begin to connect with the scale of the land, you discover details of terrain to slow you down: a bend in the river; a series of peaty ditches; the traces of a booley shelter; the stone-faced edge of a derelict levee. Whatever was wild in this landscape begins to intermingle with marks of human effort into one impression; but the place is not tamed or defused: the thoughts of people living here with their livestock, moving over this land, interpreting it with their words, giving it names – of a community bound up with the cycles of light and growth, of scarcity and abundance, all make the landscape even more a wilderness to our thinking, but a wilderness embroidered with human signs.

The walker is just the latest in a long succession of pilgrims, pastoralists, anglers and hunters who have come here and left their mark, piling stone on stone to make a boundary or a cairn, or casting flies on the river to catch a fish that would fuel an anecdote over dinner at the lodge. It was out of some general curiosity, without a definite object this time, that I went back to Tarsaghaunmore a couple of weeks later to make another foray into the higher reaches of the valley. The swallows had all gone by then, and the first redwings had arrived as a sign of coming winter; I took the sight of an otter's splashy, whiskery head in Bellacragher Bay as a good omen for my excursion.

When I got to the village, smoke was rising in a leaning trail from Paud's chimney, a sign that he was at home. The smoke made his cottage appear like a vessel on a long journey across the sea of the bog. No sooner had I switched off the engine than Paud was standing there to greet me, as if he had been told to expect me. I shook his hand; I had not seen him for a long time and smiled broadly, but he is a shy man and did not face me as we talked.

As well as seeming to materialise like an angel at the gable of his cottage, you would also think that he was reading my interests without any prompting: he immediately talked about the wildlife he had seen in the area (as the fishing season is over, that topic is dormant now). This was his wildlife report, which I set down here as precious marks in the vastness:

Red grouse are plentiful in a few places: on the Bangor Trail just south of Bangor, in Tarsaghaun just downstream from the village (a brood of eight this year), and on a ridge at the top of the catchment, which he refers to as Cruach na gCapall. His pronunciation of this Irish placename is perfect, although he does not know what it means.

He mentions hawks he has seen near his house, one with a golden head, which perches on an electricity pole. They are bigger than gulls and cause panic among the hens: I am unsure if he is talking about buzzards or an escaped falconry bird. He has not seen an eagle but knows about the golden eagle that spent time in the mountains to the south a few years ago. A woman at Bangor saw a big bird swoop down to take a cat. 'It brought a cat,' he says, 'and a cat's not easily brought.' I am delighted that eagles have again

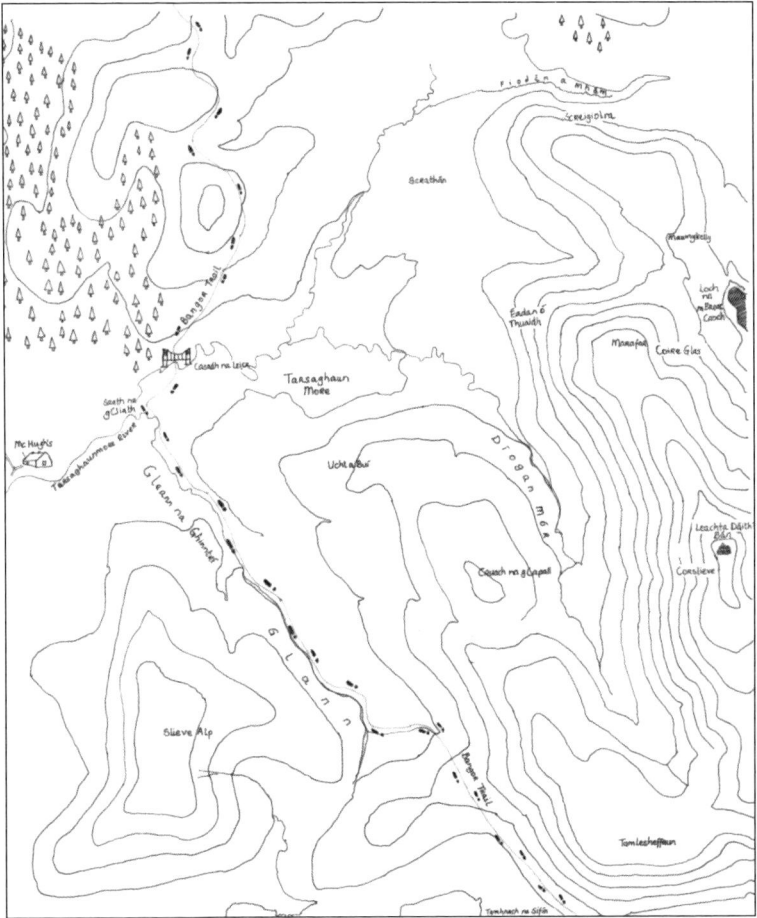

entered local knowledge, a lifetime since their first disappearance from this area.

Woodcock are common in the forestry at the approach of cold weather, he says, 'When they're in it, you know that snow and frost are coming.' He sees red deer regularly in the forestry plantations along the river: there are two stags with a herd just a mile downstream of the village. And he also saw an owl, 'a big, grey owl', one evening, which I take to be a long-eared.

I have a neighbour's dog with me today, a black border collie called Angel. Paud tethers his barking dog to its kennel as I get Angel out of the car and prepare for the outing. We go upstream and soon cross the river close to the Bangor Trail. Angel learns her first lessons in bog protocol and sinks into a few sphagnum patches as we cross wet flushes south of the river. Then we climb the hillside overlooking the trail and begin to get a panorama of Tarsaghaunmore. The river running through the bog is marked by a strip of green pasture, with a sprinkling of grazing livestock. An area of small lochans is spread out nearby, like the shards of a shattered mirror.

The double track of a quad leads up this hill, scored in the soft upland a few weeks ago when sheep were being gathered in. Three grouse rise from the heather without calling; one bird flies in a great arc in front of us, the whirr of its wings clearly audible in the silence. The quad track divides: some marks run straight up to the top of Cruach na gCapall, the first spur in a ridge that runs up to Tamlesheffaun, the south-western shoulder of Corslieve.

I keep to a lower line, with the river in view as it turns gradually into the valley of An Díogan Mór. This narrow valley is aligned along the western flank of Corslieve for about four kilometres, ending in a steep-sided bowl, not quite a corrie, just under the 500-metre brow of Tamlesheffaun. An Díogan Mór has no record of booley huts along the valley floor, and no steep cliffs or other dramatic features: its isolation and apparent lack of features are challenges I have set myself today.

After a snack and a pause to take in the silence, I continue a slow, steady trudge around the flank of Cruach na gCapall. In perfect keeping with Paud's report, two more grouse fly from heather-covered ground. The vegetation is marked by sheep that lie up on this sheltered slope during summer nights. The scree-silver shoulder of Corslieve looms above us as we move. Over that, the eternal simplicity of empty grey sky, which offers nothing to my searching eyes. I search the top of the mountain with binoculars and spot the cairn, Leachta Dáithí Bán, with its neat concrete trig point, emerging as a heap of stones in a landscape of stones.

The river in this upper level of the catchment is a young thing in a hurry, cutting a trench through glacial drift and bedrock. My map calls it abhainn gharbh, rough stream. One rowan is now clearly visible with vivid red berries emerging like a bouquet from the vase of the river's narrow gorge. It is the best waymarker I can see and I make it our lunchtime stop. This tree has a few companions, a holly and another, younger rowan growing from the sides of a rocky gorge. Floodwaters have worn the bedrock smooth and formed a deep basin, now full of ale-coloured water. Bilberry, woodrush and heather grow in profusion on the sheltered, inaccessible rock wall. The deep pool here resembles those paradise pools of tropical fantasy, but when I immerse my hands into the icy bite of this water off the mountain, I am checked by a northern reality.

Other small streams have worn deep channels into the flank of the mountain above us: each of these grooves has its decoration of rowan, now heavy with red fruit. As we resume our walk following the course of the river, there's another flat grassy srah where the water, deflected by the slope, has deposited sand and gravel. This could have been the site of a booley hut, but I find no trace in the heather and bracken. More rowan trees are ahead, each abundantly dressed with berries, their brown leaves turned skywards, like worn hands raised in supplication. A thrush flits from a tree and disappears. Then a robin pops up, hunting insects across the treetop. I think of Keats's 'unheard melody' of song in this deserted valley. The image fixed in my lens, a bird in a chandelier of red berries, is a Christmas scene two months ahead of schedule.

Something small and white is hovering among the leaves at the top of the tree: a dragonfly? The binoculars find a clump of gossamer, about the size of a matchstick, being wafted and held horizontally by a scarcely perceptible movement of air.

Having followed the stream as high as we are going to go, I sit for a while beside the hurrying water and admire form and texture in the stones heaped along the channel; my favourites are layers of quartzite, twisted by pressure and heat into elegant curves. Many blocks of red sandstone have also ended up here, dragged by glaciers from their original setting on Clew Bay.

Our route out of Díogan Mór is a shallow pass between two gentle hills. Before we turn to follow this path out of the valley, I look up to its southern end, almost two kilometres away, and reserve that amphitheatre of mountain for another, longer day.

Despite all my head twisting and gazing in search of an eagle or other large raptor, nothing appears in the empty, grey sky.

I slog up to the top of the ridge on the western side of the glen. Angel follows me obediently, close behind. As the terrain levels off, a dramatic view opens up to the west and north: the peninsulas of the Mullet and Geesala, and Tullaghan Bay – flat expanses of land with deep incursions of sea. The houses at Tarsaghaun are visible, and with binoculars I can see my car parked at McHugh's, still an hour and a half away.

I pick up the course of another fiddaun draining into the Glann, the local name for the next valley, which links the Owenduff and the Tarsaghaunmore catchments on the Bangor Trail. Another good spawning stream runs through here, heading north on its way to join the Tarsaghaunmore. Though now reduced to 'the Glann' in local usage, the expanded version of this placename is Gleann na Ghinntrí, the valley of the wedges, so called because of the appearance of a series of descending slopes and ridges forming the sides of the valley.

The vegetation here is recovering from a major burning in 2014, and appears like a gingery covering of grasses over black peat: the heather is a shorter carpet, still struggling to come through. Purple moor grass predominates across a wide stretch of the hillside and my boots hiss as they pass through its long, yellow leaves. I come upon the first expression of the fiddaun as a young stream creating sandy deposits and grassy turf in the moorland. Then suddenly, sooner than expected, I am onto the stony track of the Bangor Trail.

No one walks the trail nowadays except for a few adventurers and sheepmen. In their absence, the trail is populated by ghosts from other centuries, of people who travelled here before roads were built. A kilometre away to my left is a stream called Fiodán a' Chailín: the placename commemorates a girl who was murdered as she returned from a market in Newport; it is said that her killer failed to find the banknotes she had hidden in a plait of her hair.

The firm footing of the trail is a relief after the soft accidents of the bog and gives us smooth passage along the river through the Glann. The National Park has installed sections of boardwalk across some of the softer hollows, and there's a new bridge over the first of two so-called Black Streams. Angel and I march quickly over nailed sections of timber and step across a succession of neat drains. A great heap of sandy spoil on the far side marks the site of a badger sett.

When I come upon the first line of fencing near Tarsaghaun and see cattle in a field near the river, I feel that I am returning to civilisation. Angel senses that we are close to our destination and trots along the track ahead of me as we approach Tarsaghaunmore.

The eponymous river running through this glen is a thread connecting different histories: people who came here on ancient boolies in summer, others who opted to make it their permanent home, and a small band of researchers and fieldworkers who have surveyed this valley for different purposes over the years. To these you can add walkers who have crossed the river on their way along the Bangor Trail, part of an obscure community of visitors whose memory has been imprinted by this place, even where they have no name for it.

The river has a different and distinct identity among salmon and sea trout anglers who come here every year when water levels and the season are right. Many of these anglers are visitors to the area whose professional lives are lived out far from the open peatlands of Erris, but their angling passion brings them back here again and again to fish the pools and streams; they know the river intimately in their fishing terms, and their memories have been marked by days when the river gave a bounty of salmon or sea trout, especially the latter, for which this river is renowned.

During the summer season, these anglers are asserting fishing rights that in many cases originate with the old landed estates, and their arrival on the river is a sign of old social divisions. The people who live along the river, and who endure the harshness of its dark months, are now mostly prohibited in law from fishing here. These old relationships, between locals and gentry, are well documented in the case of Connemara by Tim Robinson, but they also exist in north Mayo's landscape of spate rivers and hunting lodges.

I returned to Tarsaghaun one November evening in the company of two men whose lives have been bound up with salmon and sea trout fishing in Mayo and Connemara.

Jean-Pierre (J.P.) Maire had just closed his café after a long summer season and was keen to get out on the terrain. His son William, a geology graduate, travelled with us. I got to know them from the café they run at the visitors' centre in Ballycroy National Park. During breaks between serving customers, J.P. tells me about his adventures during the fishing season; his wife Nicola Stronach, who runs an art gallery at the same centre, chats to me about the artwork she is exhibiting.

J.P. and William are keen and accomplished anglers who catch sea trout and salmon in unfamiliar places. They praise the attractions of fishing for Mayo's sea trout at a few secret locations along the coast, where they have taken – and released – some big, pale fish, very different in appearance from the darker specimens that we encounter on the bog streams, where the spirit and colour of peat casts a chameleon shadow.

As we drive in J.P.'s car to north Mayo, I listen to his account of managing a sea trout fishery at Fermoyle Lodge in Connemara, where he also worked as head of hospitality and catering for many years. As fishery manager, J.P. was involved in ranching sea trout at Fermoyle and in river work, including flying in gravel by helicopter to improve the quality of spawning beds in the river. Like so many others, he witnessed the impact of fish farming on salmon and sea trout stocks in Connemara. Three or four individuals, he reckons, are responsible for the greater part of the damage; if they could be paid off through a compensation scheme, he thinks, stocks would recover, and Connemara's famous sea trout fisheries would thrive once more. While veterans of the angling sector will tell you that sea trout stocks are a mere shadow of what they used to be, there are still enough in Connemara's lakes and rivers to attract anglers to these high-earning beats, along with the accommodation packages that accompany them.

William, who sits in the back of the car firing questions and intervening into the conversation, has his own stories of big sea trout up to five pounds, which he caught earlier this year on the Owenduff. The north Mayo rivers appear to be still in excellent condition principally because Blacksod Bay, which is the coastal home of north-west Mayo's sea trout, does not have any salmon farms. A small fish farm at Bellacragher Bay has had no apparent impact on sea trout and salmon stocks. The curse of sea lice infestation has spared Blacksod Bay so far.

When we get to Tarsaghaun, we pay our customary respects to Paud, who appears on cue at the corner of his cottage, looking surprised at this out-of-fishing-season arrival. Surprised too that we propose walking upstream with torches, to search the river for spawning fish in the darkness.

I am cast in the role of guide because of my experience in this area with students, companions, and on my own. Having parked the car three hundred metres from Paud's house, we get out to contemplate the river, still at a fresh, refreshing level after rain the previous day. The evening is closing in as we stride out across Sraith na gCliath towards the new footbridge. Two new concrete plinths have been installed on the riverbank to replace the old concrete cylinders that rested on the bed of the river itself; they now support a proud steel structure in magnificent isolation under the summit of Corslieve.

We continue upstream in deepening twilight. In the second pool above the new bridge, a big fish, the first we have seen, scuttles off upstream, leaving the shallows of the pool tail for deeper water. There are cattle along this section; the ground we cross is marked and pitted by hooves, and we tread carefully. By the time we reach what I consider to be the heartland of this territory, the only gleam is from the surface of the flatter pools, where an oily residue still lingers. A sea trout turns and splashes twice on this faint aftermath of evening – and we walk on. I take a short-cut across the bog to get us directly to Casadh na Leice, the largest holding pool, where J.P. switches on his stalker's lamp for the first time.

The tail of the pool is quite shallow, scarcely a foot deep, with an even flow of tawny water across gravel deposits. 'This is where they will come,' he says approvingly. No fish are visible now, but we are ten days ahead of the main sea trout spawning time, and over a month too early for salmon. My torch and head torch are ineffective at this pursuit; they do not penetrate the coloured water down to the stones, and we rely on J.P.

As we follow the stream down, his lamp pierces the gloom, like strokes of diluted tea across the river. The densely compacted areas, where stones lie in clusters like cobbles, are no good, he tells us. Fish need looser gravel where they can excavate a redd in the river bed. We follow his demonstration of several shallow depressions: 'Here, and here,' he says, pointing out a few hollows with the lamp where finer sand appears pale among darker stones. Like figures in a painting by Joseph Derby, William and I are oblivious to the great mass of night taking shape around us as we watch the beam in its brief, ephemeral revelations.

This method of night lamping reveals the river in a new way. In the glitter and glare of day, the pools and deeper streams are unfathomable; light is reflected off the surface so that the body of water itself is as dark as peat, with a mysterious and shy population of fish hidden under the grey camouflage of their upperparts. The night lamp probes these secrets: shallower parts emerge as rocky beds – only in deeper sections, three feet down or more, does the lamplight disperse as a fog in the brown gloom without finding the river's stony foundation. J.P. pointed out many shallow streams where barely a foot of water ran steadily, without much agitation, across the river bed: these are the likely spots during peak spawning time, when fish forsake the deep pools and become mesmerised by the breeding instinct. Along the flanks of the breeding cock and hen pairs, I am told, you can also see tiny parr, ready to fertilise the eggs if the cock fish fails.

Eventually, our search yields a small reward: a sea trout of about a pound, and another, larger fish close by, sitting in a current at a depth of about a foot in a pool tail, both cock fish waiting for hens. They sit steadily, apparently unconcerned by the glare of the lamp.

As we get close to the bridge, having covered several streams with the lamp, a large fish is startled by J.P.'s light and sounds a heavy kerfuffle: there in the shallows, at the edge of the beam's range, is a salmon with water washing its back, its dorsal fin proud of the flow. After its initial lunge away, it does not flee as a salmon would during the day, but it stays, already drunk on its breeding instinct and its nocturnal quest for a redd. This silver, scaly flank with a purplish shimmer, almost of phosphorescence, incarnates a whole geography of the North Atlantic, where the fish has spent at least several months since it left this river as a smolt, along with the realities of predation by man, seals, otters, and others – from which it has emerged miraculously to survive as a warrior of its kind.

Eventually the fish fades out of our vision and we do not pursue it, as poachers would.

Before our probings finish, as we stare at flowing water, we hear the noise of geese calling overhead. 'Geese!' I exclaim, which J.P. corrects with a confident, curt, 'white-fronts'.

As we cross the river again, I do a St Christopher act, using my hazel stick for support, studying the fast flow pressing against my boots to make sure I avoid wet feet. When I emerge, dry-shod, on the other side, our river quest has ended and we pick our way across Sraith na gCliath without speaking. The wings of a woodcock whirr in the darkness: a bird has taken off from a rushy area. They are arriving now on nights such as these, guided by a big moon, known in November as a woodcock moon.

Matching the moment, an almost full moon has just come clear of clouds north of Corslieve, above the ridge known as Marafar. (The name is possibly from the noun marbhacht, suggesting dead-beat exhaustion.) This braddy moon would guide us home, if we needed it. It would not, on the other hand, help our fish quest: moonlight distracts spawning fish. I am told they prefer darker nights.

J.P.'s lamp probing the murky waters of the river at night struck me as an emblem of the searcher's enquiry into this region's past. The available records such as census data, valuations, maps and estate records, tell a surface story of ownership and exchange, but they can reveal little of the lived experience of an illiterate, Irish-speaking population; and even where we manage to glean information to feed into the statistical discourse of history, there's also a deeper level of imagination beyond those so-called facts. Where recorded history fails, as it usually does faced with the extinctions and absences of Wild Nephin, folklore can supply something of the deficiency. One of the few lightbeams of insight into an older culture comes to us from a traditional Mayo song 'Rann an Mhadaidh', which was collected by Micheál Ó Gallchobhair (1860-1938). Ó Gallchobhair was originally from Kilsallagh, near Bellacorick, but spent most of his adult life in America, where he and several of his wider family settled in Chicago. His collection of Mayo poems and songs, including 'Rann an Mhadaidh', was published by James Delargy in 1940.[4]

Pádraig Ó Móráin attributed the poem to a Pádraig Mac an Leágha from Rosgalliv, near Tieranaur and believed that it dates from the early nineteenth century. Given its unique associations with the Nephin Beg Mountains, I give the entire version here in my own translation, eliding a small number of intractable obscurities in the original.

I went with my lively dog for a day's sport to Glennamaddoo,
Early on Good Friday we were hunting over the hills of Maumaratta.
The big antlered stag moved to the top of the glen, into a grassy corrie.
My dog was swifter over obstacles than the wild dog or the wolf,
He was swifter than the hawk of birds striking the air,
He would grab a salmon leaping from the river however strong the flood,
His voice was sweet on the day of the hunt. Young hound, loyal dog.
The upshot was, I lost the trail, and my dog abroad in the distance,
I did not know what way my friend had taken – he was missing,
Until I heard his sweet voice in Gleann a' Ghinntrí, distant though it was,
And however I roamed about that day, I wouldn't be happy till I found him.

I moved on up to the heights above Mount Eagle,
On I went – a bad happenstance it was – to search the valleys of the Erris Mountains.
I went astray on my journey, trying to get to Dohooma.
I was put in a boat for Clare Island, and I asked the grey man for a blessing.
I was thrown into the deep sea where no mortal could get his footing.

The sea was in a raging foam, and I nearly lost my senses,
When the magic mist came over me.
I saw a ship approaching – with only one aboard her.
He was wearing a red hat on his tidy crown,
Plain leather shoes, an undyed flannel coat,
And socks the colour of sheep's wool; his beard was combed, his hair was parted,
And he said in a surly voice in the morning as he came forward:
'Was it rebellion or the devil that took your dog to County Kerry?'
'I pray to God that's not the case,' said I,
'And if the dog's in Ireland we'll get the story from Seán Noble.'
When I came ashore the rain was at my heels and I was half drownded.
I came into a house in the hope of something to cheer me up.

A small old bony woman came after me as I was looking around,
And you would think she was pledged to the devil from the time she was young.
'Get up and leave my house, you won't be staying here with me!
Is it from Ballycroy or Achill you are, you tramp, where's your bag?'
'I am not from Ballycroy nor from Achill; had I been from such a place,
I would get bed and board there tonight with a thousand welcomes.
I frequented Tieranaur and they never turned me away,
But I'm looking for my dog that strayed from Glenlara.'

'Get up and leave my house now, and stop this contention!
And I can tell by your voice that you're a senseless
blackguard.'
She picked up the flax rippler and hit me on the brow,
And to see the mirth rise up in her came as a relief.
When I realised I was wounded by the gap-toothed,
toothless hag,
I was dismayed and put to shame to have nothing for my
pains.
Then I rose up proudly, I towered over the old woman,
And I grabbed her by her wiry hair and knocked her to the
floor.
She drove her long, crooked nails deep into my skin,
And then it dawned on me that Fionn Mac Cumhail had
refused the hag's assistance.
We were at that work until the stroke of noon.
It is many a place I wandered and never got my restoration,
And then I met that old hag, my curse on her till she dies!

I didn't stop then until I got to Crossmolina,
I saw no one alive whom I'd ever met in my life,
Except Seán Ruadh Mac Ailpín standing in the door of a
porch.
He had a loaf in his hand, with a knife and strip of meat,
And when he saw me coming he put it all away.
'Seán Ruadh Mac Ailpín, blessings to you my friend!'
Then I told him in a whisper that I was dead beat;
'There was no point in all in those foolish pursuits,' said he,
'You should have stayed at home to save on wear and tear
Instead of searching for your dog and he up on the breast of
Glen Nephin.'
'Well, Seán Rua Mac Ailpín, I wish you trials and sorrow!

To think of all the times you had food in neighbours'
houses,
And now that I'm at death's door you couldn't share your
lunch,
Well, if I was three months fasting, you could stick it all up
your arse!'

When I got up in the morning I was weak and worn out,
I searched through Glen Nephin up and down,
I searched Drogheda, Clonmel and the Joyce Country,
And, by God, didn't I rear him well, that dog with a big
snout!
He could kill a seal on the sea, and he could bring a
porpoise ashore,
He had other skills as well, he could herd goats and sheep.
When I got up in the morning I was weak and worn out,
And who should I see but my doggy and the stag beside
him,
So off they went and jigged away as far as Clare Island,
And me getting stuck in quagmires as I went trotting after.

My fine dog got him by the ear when he was driven from
cover,
Down at Srahacorick one evening where we killed him.
I stood over him to have a look and strip off the hide,
And along came Dominic Ó Méarlaigh to get his quarter.
I spoke to him and said that the priest wouldn't have it
gratis,
'A lot of men are after a portion, but I'd like to have the
sale of four.
I'll send a joint up to Ruaidhrí Mac Meanmna,
Because I'm scared to death of Tuathal Ó Gallchobhair,
If I met him all alone he would lash me with a stick!

And I'd be no trouble to finish off after all the hag has done
to me.'

And then the toothless hag spoke – without a gnasher in her
jaw.
'I'll come up with pleasure if I can manage to tear off
enough
To make a pot of broth to cure the cough.
It's a crying shame that I wasn't able to get Mártain Ó
Cheallaigh's portion!'

We'll have to get a writer with lore and learning,
To write an account of this division of the meat;
Each quarter filled a barrel as they weighed it on the crane,
And when the hide was divided out it cloaked an Irish acre.
I gave the skins to Séamus for him to do with them as he
pleased.
There was a coach and four carts to carry the head to the
knacker's,
To Mártain Ó Uallacháin, who is handy with the loy.

The geography of this extraordinary narrative corresponds
closely to this book's territory: its northern limit is Gleann
a' Ghinntrí in the catchment of the Tarsaghaunmore River;
it extends eastwards as far as Crossmolina and reaches its
western limit in references to Achill and Clare Island. Most
of the placenames can be assigned to actual locations,
although the dream-like atmosphere means that there are
sudden shifts, with places becoming a kind of incantation –
as if to evoke the broader territory itself rather than an
actual itinerary. In a process of shared reminiscence, the
audience of this poem will have heard their landscape being
invoked through its placenames, including Gleannta

Shléibhe Iorruis, the Valleys of the Erris Mountains; this marker appropriates the entire Nephin Beg Range on behalf of the barony to the west, a bias which fits well with my own better acquaintance with the catchments of the Tarsaghaunmore and Owenduff rivers. This recital of places as territorial markers takes on an added poignancy in this case when we consider that by the time the poem passed from oral to written tradition during the early twentieth century, the collector and his family were based in Chicago.

It is clear from the greedy division of spoils that the killing of a stag was a special event; when this poem was composed at some time in the early nineteenth century, deer must have already become scarce, as is suggested by W.H. Maxwell's account of the rare appearance of a red deer stag during a shoot in the Maumaratta area in the 1820s. The stag in 'Rann an Mhadaidh' was finally killed at Srahacorick, close to the poet's locality at Rosgalliv, Tieranaur; the several names mentioned in the conclusion evoke local obligations, though Pádraig Ó Móráin was unable to identify any of these individuals when he enquired among the local people in the early 1940s. [5]

William and I come back a week later to search the tributary of the Tarsaghaunmore draining the Glann. Paud is at home but does not appear this time.

Just as we set off to follow the track down to Sraith na gCliath, a full-arch rainbow spans the entire catchment ahead of us, with its right foot on Cruach na gCapall and its left in the forestry – a triumphant arch for our arrival.

A cow pat on the srah is riddled with woodcock bill marks – possibly the bird we flushed a week earlier. Two sea trout swim away up the little fiddaun you have to ford at the top of Sraith na gCliath. They were lying in shallow water, on a bed of yellow gravel, preparing to spawn.

We wade across the main river at its junction with the stream coming out of the Glann, cross a fence and a few remains of levees, then join the Bangor Trail for a couple of kilometres. On our way upstream, a few sea trout move out of the pool tails. William, who knows the peaty, silted streams of Connemara well, is delighted at this little stream with its gravelly shallows and deeper pockets.

About a mile away to the south, we can see the Bangor Trail as a seam in the bog rising up to cross a ridge forming the watershed of the catchment of the Glann. I talk to William about highwaymen and traffic on this path before the coast road was built, now the N59. William gives me impromptu lessons in metamorphic rocks, handling blocks of schist and quartzite that litter the trail along with rounded pieces of red sandstone brought here by glacial action. A soft, pale silt has settled on the trail and is marked only by animal hooves; there have been no walkers here for days, perhaps not for weeks.

The little stream, just four, or five, or six feet across, has created a narrow flood plain in the Glann between thirty and forty metres wide as it meanders through its own valley. The fine, pale, mica-rich sand flushed out by big floods lies all around on the riverbanks, and in places the ground is exposed in section by the river as a layering of fine sand with a peaty admixture. This precious stretch of well-drained pasture still has value today, allowing the creation of a few fields for grazing.

We decide to stop and switch on our lamps. We then strafe the stream with the powerful beams and paint a picture of this river with a broad lamp brush. Yesterday's brief spate has gone down, but the water is still full and fresh, moving across gravelly shallows in a steady flow — ideal habitat for spawning fish. The lamps disturb a couple of sea trout in a long, shallow pool, but most of our searching proves fruitless. Perhaps the fish, alerted by the light, dart away under the banks and stay there.

Larger blocks of dark rock combine with pale stretches of loose gravel on the bed of the stream. The green filaments of a weed, like a woman's hair, are a token of life in this inert stream; a few times we mistake a waving filament for the tail of a fish. Now and again a piece of bog oak, like the fragment of a giant prehistoric bird's foot, sticks out into the stream from a base of glacial drift. These blackish roots are known as black oak by the locals; the wood is silicified, harder than softer bog deal found at higher levels. Small fragments of mica in the gravels reflect back our lamplight as intense stars.

The clear night sky is established above us and our poachers' tableau. An occasional plane moves steadily across as a flashing point, and William exclaims when he sees a falling star. There's hardly any sound of bird or animal, just the thin note of a migrating redwing.

When we reach it again, the Tarsaghaunmore seems a big river, flowing proudly, generously over a spread of shallows just at the junction. I use my large, borrowed lamp to cross the srah and pick out, on the grassy thoroughfare, a few pale, folded miniature brollies of bonnet mushroom (*Mycena sp.*) with fine, dark seams on a milk-white, delicate cap. The night is frosty, pinching my feet with the first winter cold of the year.

Falcons at Blue Lodge

In the course of my rambles in Wild Nephin, I received an invitation from friends at Rock House to join a group of falconers on an outing hunting snipe. This was a welcome summons back to the open landscape of the Owenduff catchment on the western side of the range. The visiting members of the Irish Hawking Club would be arriving at ten o'clock on a Thursday morning to rest their birds after travelling and prepare them for flight.

My route to Blue Lodge took me past Bellacragher Bay and Claggan on a calm, partly overcast morning in late October. The forecast was promising imminent change in the weather: a front moving in from the west with cold northerlies in its wake. I turned off the main road at Bellaveeney and drove among forestry conifers where Jessica and I had seen and heard red deer a few days previously. After a right turn and a short run among encroaching rhododendrons, the road leaves the last few houses behind and sets out across unspoiled bog, as it does so diminishing to an untarred track.

This is open country similar to many Scottish flows, where gentle undulations are interrupted by the occasional surprise of open water: bog pools, locháns, and a few bigger lakes. I drove towards the main visible feature ahead, a copse of rhododendron crowding around a few stark, declining specimens of Scots pine. Peat is still being worked by hand here along a few banks; dried sods are stored by the roadside in large ricks covered in black plastic, secured with stones, old tyres, and sometimes the addition of a fine mesh of monofilament salmon gill nets. These unthinking structures have always fascinated me with their coarse, evocative artistry: typically about two metres high, and perhaps ten metres in length, they memorialise raw subsistence in the remote vastness of north Mayo. In half-earnest jest, I imagine them transported to the ritual spaces of contemporary art, to take their place with other large-scale installations.

I was the first to arrive at the small car park among the rhododendrons. Seventy metres farther on is Blue Lodge, a restored cottage that now serves as lunch stop and shelter for anglers and hunters on the sporting estate. There are just two more abandoned houses along the river here, a stone cottage from Congested Districts Board days, and a mid-twentieth century cottage which superseded it. This house stands on a slight elevation overlooking a long, eponymous holding pool in the river, a scene of many great encounters between anglers and fish. The summer fishing season was now over, its stories stored in memory, and in anglers' report sheets. The Owenduff was quiet: sea trout and salmon that had survived the sport were lying discreetly in large holding pools, waiting to spawn.

I walked around for an hour, marvelling at the quiet, inert appearance of the river in late October before spawning starts: then the first two falconers' vans appeared in the car park. As this was the first visit of the Irish Hawking Club to Ballycroy, the estate managers, Sibylle and Guy Geffroy, were there to observe, along with gillie John Noel Campbell, and myself as an invited guest. After greetings and introductions, the van doors were opened, dogs jumped out excitedly, and the falconers took their birds from their black transport boxes. In the middle of all this happy commotion, the hooded peregrines were calm and docile, perched on their keepers' gloves, a modest presence at the heart of my awe: here, I thought, were both wildness and ancient heritage being routinely unloaded from a van.

The entire proceedings chimed with Roger Tory Peterson's observation that 'Man has emerged from antiquity with a Peregrine on his wrist.'[6]

The falcons were then 'blocked' on low perches set in the ground beside Blue Lodge in order to weather them before hunting. Don Ryan, a falconer from Dublin, answered our many questions, speaking with the sanguine authority of a military officer. His birds were two males or tiercels, bred in captivity, as all these birds were. Released from their oriental hoods, they sat quietly on the chalice-sized blocks, seemingly indifferent to the noise of people and dogs. It was thrilling to be able to observe, at close range, a species that incarnates both wildness and the best skills of man at capture, breeding and training. Irish peregrines were celebrated by Gerald of Wales, in his Norman account of the conquest of Ireland, as 'the best breed of falcon'. Greatly prized by falconers, peregrines also became a flagship species during the late twentieth century when pesticide residues had ruined their breeding cycle, resulting in severe declines: by the mid-1970s, only about sixteen breeding pairs remained in Ireland. Even in the vast territories of the American West, this majestic falcon had been driven to the brink of extinction.

Out of this bleak scenario came a most extraordinary literary witness to the fascination with this species: in 1967, J.A. Baker's book, *The Peregrine*, appeared, a landmark in nature writing which would secure the peregrine's mystique with an audience beyond that of birdwatchers and falconers. Baker spent several winters in the late fifties and early sixties tracking wintering peregrines in his Essex locality on farmland and along the shores of the Blackwater estuary. His meticulous journal of observations, with its flair for insightful capture, was distilled down to a record of a single winter, and included descriptions of the Big Freeze of 1962-63. The book is a unique blend of amateur science and poetic engagement, from the statistical records of the peregrine's prey species, to the declaration early in the third chapter:

> Wherever he goes, this winter, I will follow him. I will share the fear, and the exaltation, and the boredom, of the hunting life. I will follow him till my predatory human shape no longer darkens in terror the shaken kaleidoscope of colour that stains the deep fovea of his brilliant eye. My pagan head shall sink into the winter land, and there be purified.[7]

While there is a measure of eccentric obsession and a deep misanthropy underlying Baker's quest, his single-minded pursuit of his object delivers concise formulations of extraordinary beauty. In his entry for 16th November, 'A black shower cloud was looming from the north; the peregrine shone against it in a nimbus of narrow gold.' That same day, when the bird sets out to hunt, the terror in other birds weaves extraordinary forms in the sky: 'the hawk flew faster… He fused into the white mist of the sun, and a mass of starlings rose to meet him, as though sucked up by the vortex of a whirlwind. They rushed wildly behind him, overshooting the angular bends of his flight. He seemed to swing them around in a line, shaking them out and drawing them in at will.' A short time later the peregrine flies close to the ground in pursuit of a hare: 'She clings to the rippling fleece of the earth as the leaping hare cleaves to the wind.' On 10th February, 'The shining mauve and silver woods, snow-rooted, bit sharply black into the solid blueness of the sky.'

I find it impossible now to look at a peregrine's plumage and not see it through the mesh of Baker's close-up descriptions. Baker's peregrines are almost unrecognisable from the descriptions in the field guides, many of them young birds, 'ochreous', 'tawny', with 'the sheen of autumn leaves, beech and elm and chestnut.' The black mantle and scapulars of another male 'were pale yellowish brown, flecked and barred laterally with glowing burnt sienna.' A newcomer on 13th March, also a tiercel, was 'darker and browner in colour with no red or gold in his plumage.'

Don Ryan's tiercels were frostier and bluer than Baker's youngsters: their chests were white, with a faint ochre wash, and fine, black vertical marks like the trajectory of falling stars. The white feathers of the underparts and flanks were barred with blue-black margins; the upperwings at rest were a smoky blue, with pale margins showing the dense overlap of feathers. Both wings at rest showed the edge of their linings: white like the breast, with a dense cluster-pattern of barring elaborately tailored. Each bird rested on its killing machine, the egg-yolk yellow feet appearing thin and sinewy like an old man's hands. Each bird was ringed and had leather cuffs on its legs, with a pair of cords or jesses securing it.

We chatted amiably for an hour about wild and captive birds of prey. One of the falconers, Andrew Savage from Kerry, had many stories of old gamekeeping days in the north of England, when the gamekeeper's job was ridding the countryside of vermin. 'Vermin control was the nature of the job. If it had a hooked beak, it had to be eliminated, it was as simple as that,' he said. I was concerned for the welfare of sea eagles and golden eagles, now gradually exploring the west coast. Andy assured me that the penalties for poisoning birds of prey were now severe, but he still spoke with an old keeper's disdain for the destructive ways of pine martens and foxes.

Our conversation continued over lunch, a generous spread of sandwiches and cakes on the table in Blue Lodge. John Noel regaled us with reports of the fishing season on the river, of big sea trout, and a slow year for salmon because of the long drought in June and July. Now, in late October, those tales were of a world as distant as legend. Then it was time to go hunting.

Don offered me one of his tiercels to carry and gave me a leather glove for my left fist; I was instructed to keep my hand up, if I dropped my arm the bird's instinct would be to climb up along my sleeve. The hooded falcon stirred a few times and raised its foot to scratch its head, but it showed no sign of unease at being blindfolded and given to a stranger. I made low clicking noises to reassure it as we set out across the bog.

The bog at Sraith Dúgáin, Dúgán's Srah, is a lonely stretch of blanket bog running as far as the ridge of the Nephin Beg Mountains, seven kilometres away to the east, about four to the south. I knew this area from my lecturing days, accompanying students and another colleague as we did survey transects to locate signs of red grouse.

Once they were freed from the leash, the setters worked the ground frantically, running back and forth in front of us, looking for snipe, which they locate by scent. It was explained to me that this was not like traditional pursuit falconry, but was a technique of 'waiting on', where the dogs would first locate a bird before a falcon was released.

Then a shout went up: Don's dog had set on a snipe and the first of the falcons was flying. Once off the glove, this biddable creature changed into a different energy, urgently working the air, finding its element as it circled and climbed, a dark silhouette against the grey clouds – next thing it fell like a stone, but this stoop was unsuccessful. It missed the snipe, and Don had to call it back, swinging a lure on a cord to bring it down.

By now Don, Eoghan and their dogs were widely separated on the terrain, a series of dark points diminishing on the horizon. I walked with Don and Andy, still making clicking sounds to keep contact with the bird as we trudged and toiled through soft hollows full of sphagnum moss and purple moor grass. Snipe were scarce; on the midland bogs they were encountered every thirty feet, but the dogs had to work hard to find them here.

As we chatted about falconry, the conversation inevitably turned to T.H. White and goshawks. Andy said that goshawks have to hunt and kill things every day, in a kind of chase falconry different from the carefully staged 'waiting on' that we were pursuing with peregrines. Don and I spoke about White the writer, about his falconry book, *The Goshawk*, and his brief sketch book of north Mayo, *The Godstone and the Blackymor*. We were begrudging of White both as a falconer (Don), and as a writer on north Mayo (myself), but he is nonetheless a conspicuous character, one of the few marks left by literary legacy on the open peatlands of Erris, where White was holed up at Sheskin Lodge during the Second World War. Furthermore, his reputation as a personality, if not as a writer, has been vividly relaunched recently by his appearance as a key biographical figure in Helen Macdonald's celebrated memoir, *H is for Hawk* (2014).

Terence Hanbury (Tim) White grew up in colonial India and was sent back to England to complete his education at Cheltenham. His childhood and upbringing were blighted by his father's alcohol-fuelled instability and a sadistic environment at school, where the boy endured regular beatings. In addition to this, White struggled throughout his life with his homosexuality, in an era when such drives were easily perverted into sado-masochism and arch militarism.

While he was always immersed in the natural world as an outlet for his yearnings for freedom, it was falconry that eventually gave him a key to unlock his creative life. After graduating from Cambridge, White started teaching at Stowe public school and made sterling efforts at conforming by a combination of country sports and toffish eccentricity. But within a few years he had had enough, and eventually, while on a spring fishing trip to Belmullet, he resigned from his teaching post in order to follow his vocation as a writer. At the same time, he was reading books on falconry, and came across a reference to a lost goshawk in a book by Gilbert Blaine. This bird, wrote Blaine, 'had reverted in a week to feral state, and became thereafter a myth and legend in the neighbourhood.' With its paradoxical balance of feral wildness and social renown, this formulation was a revelation for White:

> The sentence was: 'She reverted to a feral state.' A longing came into my mind, then, that I should be able to do this also. The word 'feral' had a kind of magical potency which allied itself with two other words, 'ferocious' and 'free'. 'Fairy', 'Fey', 'aeriel' and other discreditable alliances ranged themselves behind the great chord of 'ferox'. To revert to a feral state!

Having returned to England after his retreat in north Mayo, White rented a gamekeeper's cottage on the Stowe estate and received delivery of his wild-caught German goshawk in July that year. White then set about training this goshawk over the following weeks, guided mainly by an outdated seventeenth century book on falconry and his own amateurish, trial-and-error tenacity. In the goshawk he had found a counterpart to his own indomitable, excessive self. 'For someone afflicted with deep self-loathing,' wrote Marie Winn, 'here was an opportunity to ally himself with a creature even more unpleasant, uncontrolled, and aggressive than he was.'

Goshawks are accipiter hawks closely related to sparrowhawks. They hunt in woods, heaths and coverts by chasing and pouncing upon their prey, much like sparrowhawks; they are experts at sudden turns and dashes, and will even run across a woodland floor after birds and mammals. I have seen them a handful of times in Switzerland and Norway, a large, buzzard-sized broad-winged hawk at home in dense forests. On a trip to Norway in July 2001 with Jessica and my brother Liam, we were taken to see a goshawk's nest – an armchair-sized platform of sticks high in a pine tree where the female startled us by her ghostly, silent bulk.

While peregrines are fit for an earl in the hierarchy of falconry, goshawks sit lower down, a yeoman's bird. Peregrines stoop after prey in the open, performing TV-friendly air shows. Goshawks are birds of subterfuge and ambush, poachers of game leading their keeper, the austringer, across contested heaths and woodland edges. Following successful conservation schemes in North America, peregrines are an icon of rewilding; goshawks, on the other hand, are a shy, truculent species with a reputation for being very difficult to master.

When White first saw the covered basket containing his goshawk, he thought the life confined in it was 'tumultuous and frightening', as if he had confronted the essence of wildness and was taking the entire spirit of wilderness back to his cottage: 'born to fly... free among the verdure of that Teutonic upland, who now hopped up and down in the clothes basket.' After a first release into the old gamekeeper's barn, where Gos 'fled gauchely, round and about the dreary room', White caught him back and stood 'with the monster on my fist.'

White spent many hours over the next six weeks trying to subdue this bird to his will, to get it to sit on his gloved fist, to fly to him when called, and then to hunt outdoors. Again and again, the bird refused to sit, and would bate, or fly off, only to flap furiously, suspended by its jesses from the handler's arm. The cottage became 'the torture chamber, the medieval dungeon in which the robber baron was to be tormented... Gos screamed as he bated, hung twisting upside down with yell upon yell.' After many exhausting, round-the-clock sessions, White gradually made progress, despite setbacks when Gos behaved as if his austringer 'were a dangerous and brutal enemy never seen before.'

The best goshawks, he wrote in retrospect, 'were always haunted by moods and mania'; in a similar spirit, Helen Macdonald wrote that 'Goshawks are famously difficult to tame. [They] are nervous because they live life ten times faster than we do, and they react to stimuli literally without thinking.'

If White was confronting the bottom line of his own intractable character by trying to master the hawk, his experiment also had softer, even pastoral aspects. When not cursing the hawk, calling it a 'bloody little sod', 'this dolt, cow, maniac, unteachable, unutterable, unsupportable Gos', White could lapse into a Thoreauvian dream. Gos sat, perched 'in his ultimately undefiled separation' as a bearer

64

of innocence, while the writer declared, 'To divest oneself of unnecessary possessions, and mainly of other people: that was the business of life.' This nostalgic return to pre-modern purity is figured in the account, at the start of Part Two, following Gos's escape, of a great hawk fair at Valkenswaard in the Netherlands. Birds were caught here on an established migratory route, and drew hawk masters from all over Europe, 'austringers and falconers of principalities and powers.' As White confronts his grief at the loss of his goshawk, he mourns the decline of pre-modern Europe in the defunct hawk trade at Valkenswaard, 'all, like my own Gos, were gone.'

Following the loss of his hawk, the main psychodrama of this short book is over: the later parts tell of various attempts at recapturing him, and at trapping a pair of hobbies that were nesting in a wood nearby. Eventually, he gets another goshawk from Germany and hunts it successfully, but his attachment to Cully never matches the deep connection with Gos, which intensified to love at times, between bouts of frustration and exasperation.

In the febrile cauldron of the 1930s, the view of the wild that White contemplates in Gos is easily contaminated by contemporary Nietzschean impulses to power. Gos is figured as 'a wild princeling of Teutonic origin', 'a Prussian officer in a pickelhaube, flashing a monocle, who sabred citizens when they crossed his path'; at times, too, the militaristic reverence makes you queasy: Gos 'was a Hittite, a worshipper of Moloch. He immolated victims, sacked cities, put virgins and children to the sword.' Like many tradition-minded writers and artists of his day, White saw wildness as an avenue to a world uncontaminated by modernism; and he declared, 'Every falconer was an historian, a man who had found the hurly-burly of present-day lunacy to be less well done than the savage decency of ages long overpowered.' A modern political allegory comes into sharpest focus late in Part One, where Hitler and Mussolini, along with all nature's predators, are joined in a heartless contest, 'in which only one thing was right, the energy to live by blood, and to procreate.' To his credit, however, White's views never became petrified into ideology; like W.B. Yeats, these things may have been part of his imaginings, but never became part of his convictions, to use a distinction made by Seamus Heaney

In her own memoir of training a goshawk while coping with the trauma of her father's death, Helen Macdonald sums up the challenge of these birds in a passage that is informed by her biographical pursuit of White, her predecessor:

> I saw those nineteenth century falconers were projecting onto their hawks all the male qualities they thought threatened by modern life: wildness, power, virility, independence and strength. By identifying with their hawks as they trained them, they could *introject*, or repossess, those qualities. At the same time they could exercise their power by 'civilising' a wild and primitive creature. Masculinity and conquest: two imperial myths for the price of one.[8]

Macdonald's intimate memoir of the dynamics of grief and its therapy through hawking follows White's own therapeutic course as he tries to come to terms with and subdue his own 'haggard' personality. As a contemporary woman scholar, she is alert to the imperial strains in White's psychodrama with Gos, but she also has a particular focus on notions of wilderness and the wild in the early twenty-first century.

It was the idea of reversion to a feral state that arrested White and set him on the road to training a goshawk. Eventually, as his relationship with the hawk intensified, he saw himself as a 'deluded and imaginative recluse' moving away from society in the company of his bird. On a shopping trip to Buckingham designed to accustom the hawk to the sight and sounds of people, the austringer stands with his hawk, aloof from the human traffic, and returns to the house, where his 'master stooped upon my shrinking shoulder.' The following day, becoming feral with the hawk, White 'lay in the long grass at Silston crossroads with Gos on the fist.' Like most rewildings of the self, it was a temporary condition. Macdonald goes through a comparable process of detachment from human society with her trainee hawk Mabel. She writes, 'The hawk was everything I wanted to be: solitary, self-possessed, free from grief, and numb to the hurts of human life… I had to put myself in the hawk's wild mind to tame her, and as the days passed in the darkened room my humanity was burning away.'[9]

In the last analysis, Macdonald recognises the wild as an illusion. The turning point came when out hunting with Mabel, the hawk flew at her head as it emerged from concealment in a hedge, mistaking her for a pheasant. This point of total immersion, when the hunter became the hunted, leads to a turning point shortly after, as she travels home from the memorial service for her father. Fleeing to the wild in order to heal her hurt was 'a beguiling but dangerous lie.' Like White mourning the loss of his hawk, she had hoped her father was not gone but still roved out there somewhere; the wild became the other world where she might find him. This is a formula she repudiates in the book's resolution.

Among her summary formulations is the memorable statement: 'The wild,' she writes, 'is not a panacea for the human soul; too much in the air can corrode it into nothing.' And yet, this does not amount to a dismissal, especially not in an era when ideas of the wild and rewilding have again taken hold. In the Brecklands of Cambridgeshire, where Macdonald goes to watch goshawks, she surveys land reclamation and clearance, desertification and erosion and then a modern history of takeover of a landscape by military operations, turning to eventual desertion: not an untouched wilderness, she writes, 'but a ramshackle wildness in which people and the land have conspired to strangeness.' This is a formula which would serve well for the Wild Nephin area, marked, for all its seclusion, by woodland clearances, land enclosure, overgrazing, and commercial afforestation. By releasing goshawks to restore them to Cambridgeshire, or red deer and pine martens in north Mayo, 'the wild,' as Helen Macdonald says, 'can be human work.'

The modern hunter-falconers had mobile phones and GPS devices as well as their dogs and birds. Andy checked the online map on Google Earth and showed me our position, a pulsating blue dot just within the National Park boundary. Despite the wild setting, the silence was interrupted by mobile ring-tones: Eric had flown his bird but it had missed; Eoghan came back with a similar report. We regrouped and converged on a small lake where I had seen a pair of merlins on an earlier visit. They must have bred on the small heathery island at its southern end.

Eric's Irish setter was now working the ground to the east of the lake: then it stopped about ten metres from the water's edge, with its tail raised as a signal that it had found another snipe. Everyone was now keen to see a successful stoop and Eric got a few shouts to let his falcon loose to do its work. He didn't comply, however, and called the dog back; his casual, unhurried manner was designed to tease and tantalise us as well as control his animals. ('The true maestro,' wrote White, 'gives an impression of leisure and laziness in performing his feats.') After another flurry of conversation about tactics and conditions, Eric walked on towards the lake with his dog and sent it on to the point where it had set on the snipe. With the dog in position, Eric then released his falcon, a male in its second season, hatched in 2017. The bird flew off, at first apparently uninterested in the dog's position, but then it banked back, gained height, and made a few sweeping circles above the falconer, gaining height all the time. It stopped to hover above the dog, fluttering its wings in the steady current of air like a kestrel, only broader-winged, more powerful. I thought it was the moment to walk forward and put up the snipe, but still Eric held off, the falcon fell away, did another turn, and then resumed its hovering position 150 feet up. Then Eric gave the dog a signal to flush the snipe – as the bird flew up, the falcon's shape collapsed into a falling arrowhead and made contact with the snipe. It had it. Eric whooped in triumph as the falcon flew off towards the trees near Blue Lodge with its trophy. It would have time to feed before its owner called it back.

That was the only successful stoop that day but it had been witnessed by several of us and people were impressed with this demonstration of the hunter's craft. We then moved back to the lodge, Eric having gone off to recover his bird. The falconers declared themselves satisfied with the outing and the terrain: there were few fences or obstacles to interfere with the stooping falcons.

I said my goodbyes and set out along the bog track. Eoghan Ryan followed in my direction, going towards a lake near the river, hoping to fly his bird, a large immature female, at any mallard or teal that might be there. I watched him come to the top of a bluff with his two red setters, and release his falcon. It flew along a line of power lines, swept out over the emptiness, then came back and settled atop the pole between two glass insulators. I came abreast of it and could see its moustachial stripes and the white spots of its cheeks. As I moved past, the bird became a dark knob, an obscure extension of the pole, one of a line stretching all the way to Keane's, a house inhabited until the 1980s.

I did not see it move again – it just diminished as the pole diminished in the distance I was leaving, with the falconer and his dogs watching the bog lake, with the rhodos at Blue Lodge and their ailing Scots pines – all dissolving into the overcast kilometres between me and the mountains.

Every time I leave that vast theatre I move in step with the generations who abandoned the record of their labours to the bruisings of cattle hooves, the erosions of winter floods, the inexorable march of rhododendrons, and the cancellations of weather and twilight late on an October afternoon.

As if this knowledge could be mine and mine only, I was startled to be served at Daly's in Mulranny by a lady who, when I mentioned Srahduggaun, told me that her mother had been born there, at the end of that line of power cables. We chatted about the house and eponymous salmon pool beside it, sharing a complicity in a windswept secret stored within the townland name, Srahduggaun.

Jack Snipe

The Owenduff and its tributaries, including the Tarsaghaunmore, drain a great sweep of ground extending westward from the Nephin Beg Mountains to the sea. There is just one smaller river, the Bellaveeney, which stays in its own catchment to the south and enters the sea discreetly a couple of hundred metres west of the main road. The name Béal Átha Ó bhFiannaí, the mouth of the ford of the Uí Fhiannaí, points to a bygone possession of an obscure clan. Couched in a mantle of conifers, the ruins of Bellaveeney Lodge overlook the dark, sluggish waters of this estuary in a sheltered extension of Bellacragher Bay. A private fishery sign on the riverbank marks the jurisdiction and its sporting estate over angling rights on the Bellaveeney. Rock House itself is reached by turning west from here and going round the northern rim of Bellacragher Bay until you are led past a restored gatehouse by an old demesne wall. The final stretch of the avenue is a bright, airy 100-metre approach among shrubs and deciduous trees to a parking space beside the house, where, on my very first visit, our car was promptly surrounded by a brown-and-cream commotion of friendly spaniels.

The house is perched, as its name suggests, on an outcrop of rock overlooking the shallow channel linking Achill Sound and Bellacragher Bay. By the exercise of thrift, the three-storey structure with French windows opening onto a paved terrace was added between 1859 and 1862 to an older, two-tier farmhouse, which is now clustered at a lower level behind the main façade. The main statement of prestige was made here by the addition of a three-storey tower nestling just at the rear of the main building. In its present form as a sporting lodge, Rock House boasts a large basement kitchen, a modest dining room and salon on the ground floor, three bedrooms on the first floor, and an attic floor at the top. There are other rooms and offices serving the running of the sporting estate, but these are away in the huddle of buildings behind the frontage. Nowadays, the house is no longer a daring eminence rising proudly above the sea inlet, but is sheltered by the imported trees of the park. To an eye accustomed to the vast, flat distances of Erris, the grounds of Rock House are a picturesque surprise, with their mature parkland, antique shrubs and trees, and steep rocky outcrops close to the shore.

The estate originated in 1852, when Richard O'Donel of Newport House sold over 33,000 acres of land in two lots to George Clive and the brothers Thomas Jacob and Henry William Birch. This partnership oversaw the development of the Ballycroy estate over the next twenty years, with many agricultural improvements, the construction of Rock House, and the establishment of the park. George Clive, a Liberal MP and lawyer by training, had met Thomas Birch at Oxford in the 1820s. While the Birch brothers managed the ambitious home farm development at the nearby townland of Claggan, George Clive was involved in the building of the house, which became the main summer retreat for his family until about 1913. The estate finally passed from the family in 1916, when it was bought by the Congested Districts Board, and the house was eventually sold in 1936, having been unused for many years. It had narrowly escaped the arsonists during the troubled times, when a number of locals successfully pleaded with a group of republicans on their way there with a can of petrol, having earlier set fire to Bellaveeney Lodge, on 30th March 1923.

Unlike Edward Nangle's Achill mission, where proselytising zeal caused so much animosity among the local population, the reforms introduced by Clive and the Birches did not encroach on religion, although their farm managers were of staunch Protestant stock; after some initial tensions caused by the relocation of families, the farm venture ran successfully for many years and even became a model of agricultural improvement by the 1860s. A list of early tenancies from 1867 gives details of tenants, rents, acreage, and townlands, and reads like a roll-call of the most thinly populated areas of the district: Lettera, Bellagarvaun, Lurgandarragh, Owenduff, Maumaratta, Scardaun, Tamlesheffaun, Srahduggaun, Greenaun, Claggan Mountain, Drumgollagh, Kildun, Castlehill, Claggan, Tallagh, Annagh Island. James Daly and Anthony Sweeney had over six thousand acres in two tenancies comprising the entire townlands of Maumaratta and Srahduggaun respectively. The estate stretched from Bellacragher Bay in the south, to Annagh Island in the west, and east as far as Nephin Beg and the mountain lakes under the Glendahurk arête in one continuous tract. In 1864, at the annual dinner of the Mayo Agricultural Society in Castlebar, Thomas Birch boasted that 'For ten years I have tried to reclaim the wildest part of Erris. Four years ago the land was not worth a half penny per acre at Ballycroy, upon which I am now growing green crops and feeding cattle.'[10]

The Clives, Birches and their managers at Claggan had a favourable reputation in the area; their big house was not ostentatious by the standards of the time, and many locals found paid employment on the home farm in the vicinity of the house. The estate was not immune to broader political changes, however, and the land reforms of the early twentieth century eventually saw the acquisition of the tenancies by the CDB. When this transaction took place, no one was particularly interested in fishing and hunting rights, so these rights, covering over 32,000 acres of the original property, were retained by the owners of the house. This curious survival, whereby Rock House holds the angling and shooting rights to the entire territory of the original Clive estate, persists to this day, and is now a valuable asset, managed by Sibylle and Guy Geffroy for the sporting estate.

Jessica and I have spent several spring breaks at the house in the company of friends. These holidays have revolved around angling for spring salmon on the Owenduff at Srahduggaun, and they have their own rich narrative of riverbank stories involving at least three characters: Lord Lewis, Baldrick and 'the Poet'; but there has also been plenty of time for exploring the park, walking in the wider district, and watching wildlife in the bay. Although less than an hour's drive from where we live outside Westport, in terms of atmosphere and setting Rock House feels like a century and a half away. The tall windows of the salon overlook the one-hundred-acre park, where huge conifers from the original planting around 1860 now soften the impact of prevailing westerlies. As this situation is virtually free of frost, the garden has some of the exotic character you associate with gardens in south Kerry and west Cork. At spring salmon time, when the open bog is still wearing winter colours, the grounds are already decorated with the vivid hues of early flowers.

The first sign of new life is the white flowers of three-cornered leek, a plant that carpets the entire woodland floor on either side of the avenue approaching the house. While the deciduous trees are still mostly bare, with fuchsia and buddleia dormant, an early show of colour here is supplied by camellias; these pink flowers are prone to going brown quickly after opening, and by March they already look like corroded antiques. In early spring, this garden is poised between the earliest revelations of the flowering season, and the prospect of summer light: the song of a recently arrived blackcap high up in the oaks tempts you forward.

On the left, next to the terrace, a magnificent rhododendron of deep magenta dominates the small walled garden. This enclosure leads out to a larger walled field, and from here an arched gateway invites you into the main park itself. You go down a few stone steps onto a zigzag, muddy path lined with bamboo and the blades of New Zealand flax. With very few visitors and no traffic of animals, opposite-leaved golden saxifrage and lesser celandine luxuriate on the ground at your feet. By the time you get to the end of this path, you are twenty feet lower than the ground level of the main house; one more flight of steps lined with pillars of yew and overgrown with St. Patrick's cabbage takes you down to a sloping avenue known as the Broadwalk.

In an early photograph from 1870, the Broadwalk appears as a manicured strip of lawn with low shrubbery on either side; now the trees have grown tall, and the Broadwalk is in shade. The soft green flicker of early-growth montbretia runs along the borders of the path. Several ancient firs and pines compose a high canopy here, so that the rhododendrons, camellias and fuchsias form an understorey like in a tropical rainforest. The most alluring rhododendron of all is a white variety, *sinogrande*, the flowers in clusters like choirs of cherubim in their white ruffs, the female stigma extended on its style like the trout pout of cosmetically modified lips. Another rhododendron with a deep pink flower impresses with its structure of

Henry-Moore recumbent limbs big enough to supply roof timbers for a small church; this huge plant lies along the rim of a ditch carrying a small, lively stream through the grounds. Even after weeks of dry weather this little water course whispers its pleasure among the humming traffic of bees and hoverflies.

When you get to the first crossway at the end of the Broadwalk you meet one of the oldest pines close up – a great giant with deeply fissured bark carrying its own parasite shrubbery of rhododendrons in the fork of its main branches. Many big branches are dead and bark is flaking off silvery extensions, but there is still active growth at the extremities, as if this tree were now living off air and sky and not from its roots. A few smaller trees, a mature Scots pine and a feathery western hemlock, stand like acolytes beside the ageing monster.

As you walk farther into the woodland, there is more active felling and clearance. *Rhododendron ponticum* is widespread, but so are the efforts to remove it and prevent it from blocking the rides. While many stands have been planted with young pines and broadleaves, mostly oak, in the last twenty years, there's still an open pattern of older trees, and you feel as though you are in an ancient grove overlooking the sea. Eventually, the park comes to an end at a defensive twelve-foot line of rhododendron, which guarantees privacy and a certain degree of shelter at the western perimeter. In this area, the trees have to crouch down from the correction of the wind and cannot luxuriate. Some of the oak boles are contorted into spirals where the trees were not able to grow straight but had to twist and curve as they grew into the wind.

I arrived here for lunch one day in January to join a group of French hunters for an afternoon's shooting. As the sporting party were still on their way back from a snipe shoot on Annagh Island, I had time to go to the park again, finding early fuchsia, rhododendron and camellia in flower. The sky overhead was clear and there was no wind nagging at the treetops, so the scene had a feeling of self-sufficiency detached from the ordinary process of spring and summer. There was a cold, independent clarity in the heritage of the garden. Then the party arrived and I joined them in the dining room – a young man in his twenties, his father, and another man, both in their fifties. They had a few snipe and a jack snipe after their morning on the flat bogs of Annagh, a low island three kilometres long and one and a half kilometres wide between the mainland and Inishbiggle.

We converse over lunch, a large venison burger from deer shot that autumn on the estate.

Our talk turns to woodcock, which is their quarry in the afternoon. Cock arrive in numbers in the west of Ireland in October, especially on clear nights lit by a 'woodcock moon'. I have flushed several of these newly arrived birds from a rushy hillside under Nephin Beg, near the Bangor Trail. These woodland waders, which you will come across occasionally along the margins of forestry tracks, tend to sit tight by day in dense cover and move out just before darkness to feed on fields and open ground. The west of Ireland is a favourite wintering ground for the species because the lack of frost allows them to feed by probing the earth for worms and other invertebrates.

At the height of the Victorian hunting era, woodcock were being shot in astonishing numbers across estates in the west of Ireland. Sir Ralph Payne-Gallwey's book, *The Fowler in Ireland* (1882), cheerfully chronicles the scale of this slaughter. 1250 woodcock were shot at Muckross, Killarney during the winter season of 1863-64, including a bag of 850 during ten days of sustained effort by a party 'averaging five guns' led by the Scottish peer Lord Elcho. The Cock shooting at Ashford, Co. Galway, Payne-Gallwey writes, 'is among the most famous in Ireland'; in January 1879, six guns shot 350 woodcock in a week; in the same month the following year, 365 woodcock fell to six guns in four days.[11] A year later, during a spell of extremely hard weather, when starving birds were forced onto the seashore, they were 'killed by country boys stalking them from behind rocks and boulders and knocking them down with sticks as they rose.' Captain Morgan of Cork, referring to these starving country people as 'poachers', thought the numbers of woodcock taken in this way were 'incredible'.[12]

I wondered whether today's hunters are haunted by these old yarns in the way that anglers pore in astonishment over old angling records from the days of rivers teeming with salmon and sea trout. We quickly drink an espresso and then leave.

Our first foray is into the walled oak wood which you pass on the approach to the house. I am nervous about safety and protocol as we split up into two groups – father and son; Guy, the other hunter, and I. Two Irish springer spaniels, Nephin and Penny, are sent in to work the thickets. Guy, the estate manager, has kept narrow rides open among the trees with their undergrowth of rhododendrons. 'We'll keep in contact,' he instructs, implying that each group needs to know where the other is, to avoid accidents. The hunters have taken their shotguns from their cases with a care and gentleness of touch that you imagine being reserved for a loved one.

We move among the thickets as the dogs search frantically in the undergrowth. Guy keeps telling them to *cherche*, *cherche*, or calls them back if they go too far. When they are out of sight, you can follow their progress in the trembling detonations of foliage; then they emerge, muddied, wet, breathless and possessed. Only they, and not the hunters' calm, suggest that we are on a mission to kill things.

I see nothing, but hear shouts as an occasional bird is flushed, their wings striking leaves and branches as they flit away. No one has been able to line up a shot. Guy is surprised that there aren't more birds here; during wild weather this is a favoured spot.

We emerge onto a stretch of open bog where the oak woodland is fringed with gorse and rhododendron. All five of us are spread out along the woodland edge, the dogs moving frantically in the bushes – when a woodcock takes off, flying at a height of twelve to fifteen feet, and is brought down by the younger man with his second shot. The gun reports are tart and dry, quieter than the sound I was expecting, an echo from a childhood memory of a shotgun being discharged near my aunt's place at Knockbrack.

The bird crashes into the treetops and is retrieved by one of the dogs. I am squeamish about this, and wait until it is bagged, then I hold the soft corpse briefly, weighing its slender form for a moment. It seems a slight, little thing to be the object of so much effort, outlay, and expectation. With the young man excitedly sharing his impressions of the moment, we walk on – another woodcock leaves the thicket, but no one manages to get a shot in; it flies quite low along the edge and disappears again. We return to the cars through the oak wood.

The second stop is close to the cemetery overlooking Rossnafinna, a low tongue of heathery bog stretching across the inner bay. Guy instructs the father and son to cross a little field close to another bank of rhodos. Guy and I and the other man go farther along, moving past a thicket on the far side. I follow at the back, and watch two woodcock fly past, not far from the hunter, who does not shoot. My attention wanders to a greenshank feeding on the muddy edge of the inlet, and a curlew nearby. Then a peregrine appears, wheeling over us: I point this out to the others, but they don't seem at all interested. I am alone with my attention to this bird and follow it with binoculars.

We do one last fag along rhodos at the shore, just two hundred metres from the house. The light is fading as one more woodcock leaves its station, but avoids a shot: they can't get a line on the fleeing form. I realise that fowlers are just as gregarious and chatty about the events of the day as salmon anglers. Every nuance of flight, sightlines, and capture is narrated, analysed, and debated. The discussions continue over tea back at the house.

I find these men sitting in the tackle room around a bin lined with black plastic, plucking the woodcock and a couple of snipe from the day's shoot. One of these, a tiny jack snipe, is scarcely bigger than a skylark. This bird flew up, and landed again close by, in what is the characteristic behaviour of the species. The hunter walked over to the spot, stood with a dog a couple of metres away, thought he had lost it – when it flew again from his feet, and was shot. *Bécassine sourde* becomes my special martyr for today, a little icon I would found a whole belief system on.

The smaller jack snipe is the less common of the two snipe species that occur in Ireland. Unlike the common snipe, which also stays here to breed, the jack is a winter visitor from its breeding grounds to the north. About the size of a starling, the birds that overwinter on our bogs and marshes have travelled alone and at night from Scandinavia and as far away as Siberia. During their time here, they are usually nocturnal and silent, unlike the common snipe, which tears at the quiet of the bog when flushed. Jack snipe rely on camouflage, not flight, and they will sit very tight, rising only at the last moment and then pitching down again within sixty or seventy metres. It is only when they display on their breeding areas in the northern taiga and forest tundra that they find their voice, and produce a mechanical chuffing noise like the engine of a river boat labouring upstream.

The French name *bécassine sourde* implies that their silence is because of deafness; a related meaning of the French word *sourd* suggests concealment and secrecy, and this is what this species does best: on a few occasions I have risen a jack and noted where it came down, then walked forward to the spot and tried to flush it again; but I've never succeeded, not even when I had Angel, the border collie, with me running about in the same area. The bird had scuttled away, somehow. Their relative obscurity, combined with their long-distance migration from the Arctic, gives this species a very particular appeal: writing in his specialist blog on waders, Graham Appleton recorded this Blakean fascination by noting that 'For the tiny Jack Snipe, a cow's hoof-print forms an ideal pool in which to probe.'[13]

Writing in 1938, before GPS data had confirmed his hunch, Gerald Fitzgerald of Turlough House, Castlebar, expressed his reverence for 'our little visitor from half across the world'[14]; in 1882, Payne Gallwey quoted a Col. Peyton, who reported that 'It was a common expression among shooters, "I never shoot a Jack." Now I never let a Jack off, if I can help it, and have not spared one for ten years past.' The Colonel said that this was because of a decline in numbers from the mid-century, when both species were more abundant; and Payne-Gallwey believed that they had become rare after the hard winters of the late 1870s.

Nowadays, the jack snipe is still widespread in winter, though in only a fraction of the numbers of the common snipe. Recent bag returns from Irish hunters suggest that approximately one in eight snipe shot is a jack. I always count the sight of a jack snipe as a special badge on my day when an occasional one rises out of the rushes in some lonely river valley in the Nephins. And I had to suppress my sadness again recently when I joined a friend for a shoot over his local bog near Westport and watched him strike three snipe out of the skies, one of them a little jack, which I turned over carefully in my hand. The bill, I discovered, was as soft as a plastic drinking straw, not bony-hard as I imagined.

At Rock House that day, a plucked jack snipe put on the table in the tackle room was like a tiny effigy of a ballerina in pink tights. The men worked with infinite care, picking out even tiny tracts of grey down from the flesh. They would take these birds home to France at the end of the week.

Three return flights, car hire, hotel overnights, and a strict process of paperwork to secure tourist shooting permits – all for a handful of little carcasses that would fit in one handbag.

SOUTH

The View from Crimlin

A modest hill called Crimlin (186 metres), which can be climbed within an hour, offers a first view of the area to the east of the mountains, and although this account is coloured by winter, we'll go on our first brief excursion in early autumn.

Jessica and I parked at the northern end of Lough Feeagh one morning with most of the higher ground covered in cloud, and the distances dissolved within a grey mist; the land still held warmth from a long summer. A single swan anchored an absolute point of white on the grey water of the lake's northern shore.

We turned right at the start of the upper road leading back towards Treenbeg, but as soon as the sheep fence allowed, we stepped over a sagging line of rusted barbed wire and set out for the top of Crimlin. The ground on the eastern flank of the hill is heavily grazed, leaving little vegetation except for tough clusters of heath rush and bleached stalks of mat grass. The wetter hollows were packed with neon green sphagnum and a few scatterings of beaked sedge, each stem carrying the characteristic white star of its flower. There was deeper, healthier growth on the other side of the fence we were following; purple moor grass and deer sedge were already changing colour, giving a strong orange tinge to the hillside; half-way up, an area of hollow ground was blanketed deep in bell heather and bog myrtle, the latter still with lush, upright foliage.

As we went, we disturbed scattered flocks of meadow pipits and watched their twittering fragments circling over us against a dome of cloud. These fluttering silhouettes had been a mesh of song rising and falling over these spaces between March and July, but now their call repertoire was sparse. Swallows were also there, cutting low across richer areas of growth to catch flying insects. Unlike the meadow pipits, which would hold out here throughout the winter, the swallows were already gathering for the autumn migration.

We stopped at the top to take photographs and, in a ritual gesture, started a cairn where there was none, with two loose stones placed side by side at the highest point. With a view from here through 360°, Crimlin is a useful position to take panoramic stock.

To the north, the Srahmore River meandered out of the heavily planted area around Letterkeen, like a coil tethered around the pyramid of Correenmore (285 metres). Rising out of the distance, Nephin Beg, with its top hidden in cloud, was showing only the transverse sweep of its southern corrie, Coire na gCapall. The uplands to the east were a series of dark folds and pleats secured at the top by the peak of Birreencorragh (698 metres); the shoulder of its main western extension, Mount Eagle, was emerging from the obscurity, and was cut at its foot by the ridge of Buckoogh (588 metres). Between Buckoogh and Crimlin, the Western Way cuts through the heavily glaciated glen: a series of parallel lateral moraines runs here, like a set of ramparts approaching the mountain. On one of these upper corrugations, the green fields of an abandoned farm still advertise their derelict hopes to the overgrazed bog.

As we surveyed the prospects from the top, we kept an eye on the western horizon overlooking the lake, where rain was threatening. Grey cloud was brewing in Glennamong under the brow of Ben Gorm, reducing its peaks and ridges to just faint seams of grey on grey. The fine ridge of Coscéim and the steep cliff face of Poll Dubh at Glennamong were both lost in today's obscurity. The glen to our west cradled the Srahmore River on its way into Lough Feeagh; nowadays this river runs close to the foot of Torc Shléibhe on the western side. The top of this hill appeared to be draped by a brown tarpaulin above its yellow-green sides: distinctions of ownership and grazing mean that the lower slopes are heavily grazed while heather flourishes at the top.

Showers of rain blew across from the west as we retraced our steps, turning the soundscape into a loud, crisp patter of raindrops on the hood of my jacket. The ridge shaping our gentle descent was a vivid orange; the wet pallor of Lough Feeagh was stretched above that orange foreground, while at the top of this view, various tones of obscurity shifted themselves between sky and mountain ridge. As I have often done, I entertained myself by imagining these bands of colour on an abstract canvas, sitting upright on a flat surface.

However, if you leave Crimlin having only taken in the view from the summit you will miss the best view it has to offer: to get this, you need to come down onto the western shoulder just under the summit. Here you are standing at the top of the cliff escarpment overlooking the road, with a raven's-eye view of farmhouse, silage bales and shed. The present day Srahmore River is at the far side of the eponymous srah; an older river channel still twists through the fields at your feet, with a crop of willows and alders standing in a stillwater glitter. Despite the best efforts of modern drainage, the srah is prone to flooding, and some trees near the little Catholic church stand in a permanent mirror of water.

This feature gives a clue to explain an old name for Lough Feeagh, transcribed as Lough Rafarn, from the Irish Loch Shraith Fearna, the lake of the srah of the alders. The name underlines the wetness of the valley bottom, alder being a species very tolerant of flooded ground. The cryptic anglicisation, Lough Rafarn, turns up as early as 1752 in the Irish journal of Richard Pococke, the first traveller to give us a visitor's view of the area.

Pococke (1704-65) was a Church of Ireland clergyman, originally from Hampshire, whose family connections had secured him church appointments that gave him plenty of time to pursue his private interests. While still in his twenties, just after he had gained his doctorate at Oxford, he set off on an extensive tour of Europe; his detailed journal of this trip is framed as a series of letters to his widowed mother, whom he addressed as 'Dear Madam' or 'Honoured Madam'. Following a three-year tour of the Continent, Pococke left again on a second extensive tour, this time going as far as the Levant and Egypt. His two-volume account of this trip, with detailed plate engravings of antiquities, was published in 1743 and 1745 as *A Description of the East and some other countries*; it secured Pococke's reputation as an antiquarian traveller.

His European and Near Eastern travels were part of the tradition of the Grand Tour, a kind of finishing school for well-connected British gentry. The educational aims of the Tour – to view the antiquities and sights of central and southern Europe – were always hedged round with other attractions, narcotic and erotic, so that the returning young men usually had gathered more experience than views of Venetian architecture and Renaissance statuary. In order to reassure worried guardians, Richard Twiss advised, in an Appendix to *A Tour in Ireland in 1775*, that they 'can always stop his credit with his bankers, in case he behaves improperly.' Twiss estimated that the cost of a Tour came out at 'about eight hundred pounds per annum', and added that 'the cost of pictures, books, statues, etc. which the traveller may be willing to purchase is evidently not to be included in the above sum; neither any extravagances from gaming, or expenses incurred from intimacies with women.'

These kinds of anxieties might explain why Pococke took to such detailed journal keeping from the start, as a guarantee to his widowed mother that he was spending his time profitably. This meticulous habit came to full fruition in his magnificently illustrated and carefully documented *A Description of the East and some other countries* (1743 and 1745), a work he was never again to match, as the bulk of his later writings remained unpublished in his lifetime.

We get some intriguing views of Pococke on his return from the Near East, in 1741, when he stopped in Switzerland to explore the glacier at Chamonix. In Geneva he joined forces with William Windham, who was also on a Grand Tour, and whose wild behaviour was the despair of 'his exasperated father'. Windham's taste for adventure matched Pococke's appetite for novelty ('a union of patriotic muscle and curiosity' in Simon Schama's blustering phrase[15]), and the two went on a pioneering expedition to Chamonix to see the river of ice. This is the moment of Pococke's appearance in Robert Macfarlane's history of mountaineering, outside 'a little laager of white tents' pitched among fields of ripening corn near the small town of Sallenches. The unusual sight of well-to-do travellers was attracting a growing crowd of locals:

> The young man whom the locals had come to see would push back the heavy canvas flap of one of the tents and take a turn about the campsite. He was swathed in the tight turban and voluminous robes of a Levantine

potentate, and at his waist hung a dagger whose curve rhymed with that of his exorbitant slippers.

We have an independent, memorable record of Pococke's eastern costume in a contemporary portrait by the Genevan artist Jean-Etienne Liotard, now hanging in the Musée d'art et d'histoire in Geneva. The image is remarkable in that it explains, if it does not vindicate, Macfarlane's somewhat dismissive characterisation of Pococke as a showman, or 'pseudo-sultan'.[16] Pococke's stare in this portrait is that of a man whose mind is teeming with impressions of his recent eastern travels, and plans for journeys to come. The robes are parted carefully to show the detail and layering of his dress, as if for anthropological record. The fractured plinth he rests his elbow on is a token of eighteenth century antiquarianism, reinforced here by the book he holds, with his forefinger marking the page he has just perused. His credentials as a traveller are underlined in the background by the boat traffic at the port on Lake Geneva.

While Pococke's account of his Irish tour of 1752 was not published until 1891, his wide-ranging description of the country reflects both his antiquarianism and – in embryo – the emergence of a romantic picturesque tradition. For four months, from late June to early October, he toured the Irish coastal counties in an anti-clockwise direction, reaching north Mayo at the end of July. On 5th August he set out from Newport to reach the Mullet via what is now known as the Bangor Trail through the Nephin Beg Mountains. His itinerary took him along the eastern shores of Loughs Furnace and Feeagh, thence to Letterkeen and the beginning of the foot track. Today's walker who parks in Letterkeen at the Carroll bothy, crosses the footbridge, and sets out along the Bangor Trail, will soon reach the height where Pococke paused to write in praise of the scenery:

> Here I found myself as in an Amphitheater encompassed with high Mountains which made a very Romantick appearance. To the east Bockwoth and Billing Carragh to the north Carnen, and west of that Mamarakty and of that little Nefin. To the west Crooknegrah (sheep mountain) to the south Furcleogh.[17]

The term 'Amphitheater' resonates with the classical amphitheatres he had visited during his earlier European and Near Eastern travels. The word 'romantick', which is here so new that the spelling is irregular, shows that the emotional, subjective reaction to landscape is about to become mainstream, soon to explode into prominence as the romantic sublime, a term destined to become common currency following its launch in 1757 by Edmund Burke's *Philosophical Enquiry into the Origin of Our Ideas of the Sublime and the Beautiful*. 'Sublime' would displace the earlier terms 'curious' and 'curiosity' as a marker for the observer's attention, and registers the transition from a scientific to an aesthetic way of seeing.[18]

Although Pococke was not inclined to emotional rhetoric in his responses to landscape, all the elements of romantic taste are present in his preferences for scenery, such as his detailed account of scenery at Glenarm in Co. Antrim ('the most beautiful and romantick ground I ever beheld').[19]

As he looked west from the Bangor Trail towards Achill he admired the sequence of mountains running all the way to Claggan, and had this to say about corries, several decades before the influence of glaciation was recognised: 'These mountains about five one beyond the other have a very Curious aspect, the tops of most of them appearing with escallop hollows in perpendicular broken rocks'. Although he had seen active glaciation at Chamonix, the legacy of ice in shaping the Irish landscape would not be recognised until the 1820s on foot of Scottish research.

It was characteristic of the developing taste of the age that, wherever cliffs, woods and mountains provided a gradation of scenery, as in the parklands at Cushendun in Antrim, the viewer was satisfied. At Scardaun, close to the Corslieve Massif, Pococke admired 'a glorious view of the mountains of the isle of Achill, of the sea, and some fine mountains to the North east'; on the other hand, once he and his party had crossed Tarsaghaunmore, 'a mountain torrent', and were confronted with the flat, open tract of bog to the west, 'a morass extending to the sea', he despaired at 'The most dismal looking country I ever saw, the greater part irreclaimable'.[20]

The romantic taste for scenery was repelled by open vistas such as the bog of Erris. With its foundation in the sublime and the picturesque, eighteenth century taste responded to landscapes showing a variety of features and elevation, and not to just any untamed tract of wilderness. The opening lines of Wordsworth's well-known poem 'Tintern Abbey' describe a scene that is structured from the domesticated foreground to the wild, remote background, repeating a template used many times by painters and illustrators throughout the period. Following a day walking in the Wye Valley with his sister Dorothy, Wordsworth wrote:

again I hear
These waters, rolling from their mountain springs
With a sweet inland murmur. – Once again
Do I behold these steep and lofty cliffs,

Which on a wild secluded scene impress
Thoughts of more deep seclusion; and connect
The landscape with the quiet of the sky.
The day is come when I again repose
Here, under this dark sycamore, and view
These plots of cottage ground, these orchard tufts,
Which, at this season, with their unripe fruits,
Among the woods and copses lose themselves.

This gradation, from 'steep and lofty cliffs' in the distance, to 'plots of cottage ground' in the foreground, is strategic in the romantic period as it connects a fruitful, secure human community to the dramatic wilderness. The open moorland contemplated by Pococke as he approached Bangor Erris offered no such assemblage of elements to the visitor's eye: the bog was apparently unproductive, it was not anchored in any sublime drama of cliff, cascade or summit, and its wet surface would be an obstacle for horses, goods and travellers. These aspects of the moors of north Mayo have meant that the region has been less favoured by tourists than Connemara or Killarney, where the landscapes are more compliant to popular tastes shaped by the romantic period.

In his excursion across Rannoch Moor in Scotland, which he describes in *The Wild Places*, Robert Macfarlane reflects on the distinct character of blanket bog and notes that 'We have tended to exercise an imaginative bias against flatlands.' Flat terrains such as tundra, moor and flow country, he argues, 'seem to return the eye's enquiries unanswered, or swallow all attempts at interpretation. They confront us with the problem of purchase: how to anchor perception in a context of vastness.'[21] The archaeological view imagined by Seamus Heaney, who considers the issue in his bog poems and conducts an excavation of peat layers, can only be part of the response. A wider answer to the problem, I believe, lies in actually going out and encountering the ground. Like Macfarlane's Rannoch Moor, the flow country of Erris offers much more variety to the walker than might appear at first. There are many mountains, cliffs and cascades to be discovered once the visitor has overcome the initial challenges of actually getting to them.

Having reached the valley of the Owenmore near Bangor, Pococke stopped in the cabin of a local family, where he was generously entertained with 'new milk, eggs, butter and oat cake'. Given the poverty of these people, he felt bound to share his own food with them, and to give them some money as he left. He noted that 'The common people of the country live too much on these wretches when they travel, seldom bringing anything with them'. This note reminds us that, while Pococke's journal is the first account we have of tourism in the Nephin Mountains, the 'common people' had been travelling this mountain trail in some numbers for centuries. When he returned along this route three days later after a tour of the Mullet Peninsula, his party was joined by several others on their way to the fair, making in all 'a little caravan of about seventeen horses.'

At the top of Crimlin I imagine this caravan passing beneath me on its way to Newport, the drovers and handlers in steady concentration, keeping the stream of horses in check. The direct route from here down to the road is rocky and steep, but it can be negotiated with care, as I did one afternoon in mid-December, having walked up the slow, gradual slope from the south, watching hooded crows, ravens and big gulls turning in the air above the escarpment. It was a calm, clear day, with an intense, low sun reinforcing the old field divisions with shadow.

The boulder-strewn slope under the cliff is densely covered with young rhododendron, and these shrubs provided me with handholds for some tricky steps in the descent. Then I heard a soft, feeble note coming from the slope farther down, where stands of bracken had lost their leaves and gone over to a bare stubble. The sound was repeated persistently and seemed to shift, like the sound of a grasshopper warbler or a cricket. I crept down to get closer, but couldn't see anything; then it came again from another point twenty metres away. Had the bird flown off at my approach? I heard it again, very close. Was this some insect that starts a territorial display of sound on sunny days in December, another case of winter life? Other calls were answering all over the slope. Finally, my eye focussed on the sound at my feet: two dry stems of bracken were rubbing together and squeaking, pushed gently by the insistence of wind. All these stem noises together made up a low chorus of the December hillside, like the residual music of crickets in Derek Mahon's poem 'Tithonus', 'dry sticks/Straining their lights.'[22]

Without traffic or machine noise, the air at Srahmore that day was quiet, allowing this kind of hearing. On calm days in winter, silence is like a chord strung by a listener's attention, playing small sounds: the tearing note of a rising snipe, a pipit's thin call, old bracken stems rubbing in a slight breeze, the 'prook' of a moorhen in the narrow mangrove of an old arm of the river.

The Valley of Swampy Hollows

Like many before him and after, Pococke and his retinue headed up the valley past Lough Feeagh towards Nephin Beg, to join the Bangor Trail at Letterkeen. However, at the north-western end of Lough Feeagh, partly hidden by Torc Shléibhe, a valley extends like a wide dish into the mountains. Glennamong (Gleann na Muinge, the valley of swampy hollows) offers many insights into the history of this area, going back to prehistoric times. Its strategic position, close to yet hidden from the main thoroughfare, had an important value as recently as the Troubles, when republican paramilitaries found shelter in its seclusion.

Every year on the first Sunday in September, people climb up the side of Torc Shléibhe to a mass rock at Carraig an Amharc, the rock of the view, where mass is celebrated. For those who don't wish to climb, the service is relayed live to a television in the little Catholic oratory at Srahmore. The local family whose land is crossed by the pilgrims put on a spread of tea and boxty for the occasion. In 2012, a large steel cross was erected at the rock and it now advertises a sense of staunch identity and devotion to the valley of Lough Feeagh.

Jessica and I came past the little oratory recently while cars were arriving and preparations were under way for the mass. Earlier rain was clearing and a small ant-line of climbers was visible moving up towards the cross. I understand the native piety that keeps this tradition alive, but passed over the opportunity to join the worshippers. 'Forty-five winters off the land' – to adapt Derek Mahon's phrase – has taken me too far from the faith that I was brought up in.

My rambles in Glennamong have been occasional, alone or with one or two companions. I drove in there one morning in late February when high pressure had settled the weather after a dismal winter of rain and storms. The road into the glen around the foot of Torc Shléibhe diminishes to a forestry track and you have to stop to open a sheep fence before you can proceed. Then the track curves to the right as it enters the glen and overlooks the meandering stream running out of the glen into the lake. There are still the remains here of a few stone cottages, and the outlines of fields constructed from the bog using sand and gravel from the outwash of the river.

Following the river upstream, the road soon comes to a new concrete bridge built by the foresters a few years ago to take heavy lorries for the first felling of the crop. By my count of rings, the first plantings were in the 1970s, when the Northern situation was at its worst. The plantation covers the entire floor of the valley west of the river up to the 200-metre contour. It comprises the usual staples of lodgepole pine and sitka spruce, with a few stands of larch. Just across the river from the bridge, a ruined cottage with its outbuildings now finds itself deep in a grove of mature larch trees; at a casual glance, you might think that the cottage had originally been sited in the shelter of trees, but of course it was the foresters who came later and planted saplings around the old homestead with no regard for the memory of the occupants.

When I had parked near the bridge, I set out across the bog towards the slope of Torc Shléibhe. I was going east, away from the plantation, hoping that by climbing I would get a new perspective on those conifers. The spongy ground had already dried out somewhat after the abundant rainfall of that winter. Still, there were countless little streams and trickles of water adding to the noise of the river, all amounting to a vast, diffuse sibilance echoing off the slope. The only break in that soundtrack was the rush of air in ravens' wings as birds flew past.

As the slope took me higher, Lough Feeagh appeared foreshortened, as if the lake surface were spread on a vertical, not horizontal, plane, a curious effect of hazy atmosphere – which Paul Henry captured in his early morning studies of Killary Harbour. The lake was now shaped roughly like a map of England, with the bay formed at the mouth of the Glennamong River like the bulge of East Anglia. In the calm, slightly hazy air of midday, the deep-pile carpet of conifers stretching below me was a yellowish green. Several areas had been clear-felled in the last few years, leaving gaps and wide clearings among the dark stands. Close up, these wrecked and sterile spaces are like a no man's land from some First World War scenario. From a distance, the abandoned lines of brash form a pattern like the rough weave of a doormat; where these areas are replanted, new lines of saplings appear as a dark pinstripe across a warm, brown tweed.

Close to the top of the hill, a sheep fence runs across the ridge, keeping the walker away from the summit cairn, a neatly stacked affair with several quartz blocks on top. The lonely call of a golden plover haunted the sky for a while, an early bird tempted up to that summit in search of a territory. I also came upon a precious find: a pile of fresh grouse droppings where a bird was roosting under a low peat bank. Just past the summit, a pile of old, abandoned fenceposts gave me the struts to build an improvised stile and cross the fence.

That day I was looking for a cliff marked on my map as Carraig an Iolra, eagle rock, an old breeding site on the northern side overlooking the bothy at Letterkeen. Twenty minutes of searching along the steep edge of the mountain brought me to an escarpment with deep heather and sheer rock faces. A few ravens had quartered the cliff and were turning in the emptiness below me. This was still sheep territory, but there were many corners and ledges where heather grew in profusion as a reminder of what these hills would look like if the pressure of grazing were removed. I scrambled down as far as I could, across woody stems of flattened heather, to get a view of Carraig an Iolra, an inaccessible bluff on the face, with a secure ledge in deep growth – the perfect setting for an eyrie. From here, golden eagles had a commanding view of mountain, moor, and flow country to the north, before this tract of country was forested.

The most spectacular views of Glennamong are to be had from its northern rim, under the 628-metre peak that has an uncertain name. All three questionable names marked on a recent map refer to lower features (a pass, a corrie, a glen) and not to the peak itself. In the absence of any certainty here, by way of personal tribute to a dog that accompanied me on an excursion to this high point, I'll refer to it instead as Angel Mountain. Just off this peak you look down into the smooth bowl of Coire Hob which hangs above the forestry line. From there you see an impressive 200-metre cliff rising out of Poll Dubh in the north-eastern corner, and Ben Gorm, almost four kilometres away, rising steeply off the ridge like a camel hump. My walk to the foot of this hump began at the new forestry bridge, where we must start from.

I arrived there early one morning in January as the first blush of sunlight lit the rocky flanks of Ben Gorm, with the glen itself still in shade. The moraine under the peak was like the flank of a sleeping monster, its soft ginger tone woven from deer sedge and mat grass. The summits were clearing, but scarves of cloud were draped over the tops. A few smoky, buff-coloured clouds were drifting northward. To the east, the sky above Buckoogh was a butter-coloured wash; molinia around me was straw-pale, gathering discreet light before the glare of the sun's appearance would burn out its homely colour. Then the sun edged above Buckoogh and light reached me in a tidal shift; I felt that the morning was going to be lost in a flood if I did not hurry and get out on the ground.

This time I parked beside the bridge and scrambled along the far side of the stream to avoid entering the plantation. Several fences and deep growth made for heavy going, but eventually I got onto the slope leading up towards Ben Gorm. The ground here is very degraded, with mat grass like pale, spiky sea urchins on the dark peat. Then I heard the noise of running water and came upon pipes and tanks gathering water from the rocky ground higher up; a pleasant little stream off the mountain reaches the edge of the trees here.

I climbed on, keeping the edge of the plantation to my right as the sound of water faded away; eventually, I rounded the top of the plantation and could turn north across open ground. With morning sunlight behind me, I had an excellent view of the pines; calls and songs of crossbills were clear, almost uncontested in this place. These birds were still jittery, as if this navy-jacketed man had a gun and were after them. Eventually, I saw one perched on the tip of a pine and got a view of the bill, the mandibles crossed like a secateurs. The bird, a female, had a yellowish breast; farther on another carmine-pink crossbill was singing in the calm brightness of this January day. I crept along the edge of the trees and finally got a close view of this male in full sun, in full voice, just thirty metres away.

I was distracted by a large boulder out in the open, about fourteen feet high. When I took out my phone camera to take a picture, the internet browser announced 'Trump inauguration', so on the last day of Barack Obama's presidency, I named this rock at OS grid F 933018 'Carraig Obama'.

Then I continued climbing towards the pass, Mám a' Chaorthainn (pass of the rowans); a flock of about fifteen meadow pipits shifted about on the rocks above. The mám is a saddle at about 350 metres. There are no rowans here now, but these trees are abundant on similar slopes overlooking the lake at its southern end, so they must have grown here in profusion before most of this area was stripped of its native tree cover. As I stood on the ridge in a refreshing wind, among shifting screens of cloud, the arête of Coscéim in the next valley gradually emerged from the vapour; Ben Gorm was to the south; Cnoc Scealpach (splinter hill) was directly to the north, with the highest summit, Cor na Binne, beyond it. I followed the ridge of Mám a'Chaorthainn to get a photo of Cnoc Scealpach. Just past Cnoc Scealpach there's a sheer fall into Poll Dubh, the corrie at the very top of Glennamong. This morning, mist trapped in the dark hollow of the corrie was gradually rising clear of the bright ridge, like steam from a cauldron.

I turned away from these dramatic distances and came back down the slope towards the forestry, returning to the smaller scale of crossbill calls in the conifers. At this point, about half-way up the glen, there's a stony ridge cutting through the plantation, with stunted pines on either side; a combination of poor ground conditions and thin soil has created variety in the monoculture. Having checked my path carefully through binoculars, I entered the plantation and followed this feature, until the illusion of wilderness ended in another area of clear-felling; my last three hundred metres to the track was the usual obstacle course of brash, pine stumps and sphagnum until I got to the ease of the track.

Just where the ridge ended at the clearing, I noticed browse damage to a few trees caused by red deer; then, in a muddy patch on the track, I came across a hoof print as long as a credit card; on some harder stretches of the surface, these marks showed as V shapes in pairs where an animal had passed, running. This was my first evidence of deer in this glen.

The final stretch of my walk was a two-kilometre descent to the forestry gate where I had parked. Torc Shléibhe was glowing in the afternoon light of a low sun coming down to the right of Ben Gorm, as if it were going to settle in the crook of the mám.

Glennamong has another, antiquarian treasure: to reach it you have to start again from the bridge at the forestry gate and head for the corrie under Ben Gorm. I first went there one summer's evening with two experienced walkers, John O'Callaghan and Tom Dempsey. Tom drove his sleek VW van at a vigorous pace around Lough Feeagh and parked up just one hundred metres past the bridge, in a forestry lay-by. We stepped out of the lay-by, crossed a forest clearing, and entered a narrow section of plantation, before emerging near the concrete tank of the water scheme. Our brisk walk up the slope was enlivened by the banter of these men who know the locality well, and who have a fund of stories about the living and the dead.

After nearly an hour's walking, with the plantation to our right, we got onto a succession of rocky ridges just under the lip of the moraine. These led to the moraine itself, and the impressive jumble of rocks fallen from the side of Ben Gorm. Where these rocks became detached from the corrie wall, they left large faces or sections of bare rock on the cliff overhead. The Srahmore people, who look at the mountain from this side, refer to it as Sceilp Gorm, blue rock, whereas people who live on the western side refer to it simply as Ben Gorm, blue peak.

Tom took us nimbly across a lower section of the boulder field to the base of a huge rock, strapped on a head torch, and disappeared through a narrow entrance. John followed him eagerly, and on this occasion I was left miserably at the entrance, having succumbed to a bout of claustrophobia. I peered timidly into the interior of the chamber, as my two companions moved about on their hunkers, pointing to the spot where human bones were found in 2016. The discovery was made by a local man, Michael Chambers, who lives nearby in a house at the foot of Torc Shléibhe overlooking Lough Feeagh. Michael is a great explorer of these hills, immersed in the folklore and history of the area, and a former athlete of considerable prowess. As well as walking and climbing in the region, he also swims in its lakes and rivers, and it was one day, after a swim in Lough Doo, under the summit of Ben Gorm, that he noticed a fox on an upper slope, watching him intently. When this animal set off towards the boulder slope under the mountain, some instinct impelled Michael to follow it, and this led him to the eventual discovery of the large boulder and its hidden chambers. Michael's first discovery, of a twenty-metre corridor beside a large, truck-sized boulder, stimulated his curiosity about the feature, and on a subsequent visit with others, he discovered the enclosed boulder chamber with human remains, including broken skull fragments. The authorities were notified, and a full forensic and scientific survey was carried out. Radiocarbon dates and archaeological excavations led by Dr Marion Dowd of the Institute of Technology Sligo revealed that this chamber was the site of grave rituals for several centuries from the middle of the fourth millennium BC.

In order to give this extraordinary place its due, I have to go back again, this time with Jessica, and overcome my silly fear.

We returned one Sunday in September, during a brief gap in the autumn procession of rain and clouds. The slope taking us up to the corrie was wet from showers, but the peat was still firm underfoot following the summer 2018 drought. Some of the ground here is a case study in grazing pressure, with bleached, spiky clusters of mat grass; but there is another lesson here too, in the history of landscape, taking us back to the time of those farmers of the fourth millennium BC, and earlier. Where vegetation has been grazed and trampled away, the thin layer of peat is washed out in places to reveal the debris of glacial deposits: whitish lumps of schist on a white sandy sediment. Jessica, who hates this desolate ground, declared it The Horrid Hill – I could see her point, but was too fired up by Neolithic dreams to agree.

This area, like much western blanket bog, is stocked with the record of ancient woodland. As we walked, we saw roots, stumps, and even old branches of Scots pine revealed by peat erosion. Some of these trees at Céide Fields in north Mayo have been radiocarbon dated to the fourth and third millennium BC, and align nicely with the dates for the human bones in the boulder chamber; however, pollen

records from a lake near Lough Furnace record pine as far
back as the end of the last glaciation; it has been a major
component of woodland in Burrishoole since 8000 BC, and
was probably the dominant species on higher ground.[23] The
people who walked to the corrie under Ben Gorm moved
through a wooded landscape as they climbed, just as we
walked among the ghosts of ancient pines. Many tree roots
sat on a layer of peat, corresponding to what landscape
historians call the pine flush, a period of expansion of pine
on the peat surface around 3000 BC. We also came across
roots emerging from the base of glacial drift under the peat
layer, so these trees must have been much older.

Some of these pine fragments are wonderfully textured
with a dense grain of growth rings on twisted and knotted
sections. One piece I have on my desk shows eight growth
rings across one centimetre: this was a bonsai tree, growing
very slowly on poor ground in sub-arctic conditions; even
much larger trees, whose root plate is well preserved, grew
at a fraction of the rate of modern forestry conifers in
nearby plantations, where forty years gives you a mature
bole over two feet in diameter. The only modern conifers
that at all resemble their ancient forebears are lodgepole
pine dwarfs barely surviving on the poorest ground, in a
similar bonsai form, in a few patches of the Glennamong
plantation, and elsewhere.

As we moved up the slope, thinking we had left these
ancient groves behind, another cluster of pine stumps
appeared in a sheltered hollow at about 250 metres: this,
evidently, had not been a dense canopy forest at this
altitude, but a scattered woodland. Then we got onto the
rocky ridge and came to the top of the moraine. The talus
of boulders is spread across the face of the corrie from
about 350 to 450 metres, with the main peak at 582

metres. The main boulder over the chamber is recognisable with a sheer vertical face on the right, and a succession of frowning horizontal ridges on its brow. There are many pitfalls among the boulders here as you approach; a sheep carcass in one of the gullies was a reminder of the dangers of this ground.

When I found the chamber on this occasion I wriggled across the rock narrowing the entrance and got in easily. The ceiling of the chamber, formed by the base of the rock overhead, is slightly concave, about five feet high at its centre. The floor of the chamber is like a roughly cobbled, but still quite compact surface. I probed the corners with the beam of a torch and could see one side-chamber on the left, a narrowing shaft several feet deep. There are also two small openings at the far end, allowing a few gleams of daylight to penetrate: one of these was low down, enough to allow a cornered fox to escape; the other faint intrusion of light through a slit higher up reminded me of the light box at Newgrange which admits the sun's rays around the winter solstice. Some of the rock surfaces around me were wet, with a coating of silt that had been washed down during recent rains, but the floor itself was dry. The impression was of shelter and protection from the elements outside. I had a cursory look at the rock surfaces to search for marks or carvings, even though I knew that the archaeologists and surveyors had checked here carefully, without success. The only sign of human presence was a cluster of modern tea lights on a ledge that someone had lit as a mark of respect to the people whose bones had been brought here as part of grave rituals during the Neolithic period.

Following Michael Chambers' discovery of this chamber in August 2016, the interior was excavated by Marion

Dowd. A pit in the centre of the floor contained bones and bone fragments of several children and adults; bone remains were also recovered from the shaft on the western side and from two small side pockets. When bone samples were analysed using carbon-14 dating, the earliest date came from a fragment in the west chamber, in the range 3620-3350 BC. Another bone fragment from a side pocket yielded a similar date, while a sample from the central pit produced a reading between 2860-2495 BC. No artefacts or grave goods were recovered, but several pieces of white quartz had been placed ceremonially with bones in the central pit. As there was little evidence of burning it appears that these disarticulated bones were of bodies that had been deposited in the chamber in order to decompose, after which they were broken up or removed.

These dates put this ritual activity squarely in the Neolithic period, which began in Ireland around 4000 BC, with widespread evidence of tree clearance and some cultivation from about 3800 BC. Evidence from the well-documented area of north Mayo at Céide Fields shows farming activity from about 3700 to 3200 BC, when the famous field walls were built to enclose areas of pasture. The first phase of farming in the early Neolithic is also recorded from pollen studies at Lough Sheeauns in north-west Connemara, though here it lasted for perhaps just three centuries.[24] During the latter part of the Neolithic, peat formation spread across western Ireland and pine also colonised large tracts of bog – the so-called pine flush. Woodland regenerated where there had been widespread clearance earlier and the landscape seems generally to have been extensively wooded, even in areas with settlement and farming. A pollen core taken from a small lake near Lough Furnace gives us a glimpse of a landscape that was still extensively wooded with pine, oak, alder, hazel and birch during the period of rituals at the Ben Gorm chamber. At that time, Lough Feeagh, the wooded lake, would have matched its name, though when these hill pilgrims of the Neolithic had reached the boulder chamber, they had a commanding view of higher peaks and ridges above the tree line.

The Ben Gorm chamber belongs with the megalithic tombs that are such a feature of the Neolithic period in Ireland, which spans the fourth and early third millennia BC. The boulders in the talus of this corrie are the biggest of any scree deposit in these mountains, and are outdone only by detached sections of sea cliff around the coast. They fully deserve the term megalith, a coinage from the Greek words 'megas' and 'lithos' meaning big stone – and dwarf in size any of the boulders used in man-made tombs of this period. Here, the grain of rock is such that some chunks have split along a clean plane, leaving flat faces on the rock above, the Sceilp Gorm. The side of the large boulder above the chamber is as precisely flat as any man-made structure – the brow of the boulder presents a sequence of architectural ridges worthy of Libeskind.

Here, as you wriggle through the narrow gap between lintel and sill, it is as if you are returning to the earth, or re-entering the natal womb. To get this effect, other megalithic tomb builders raised enormous mounds and cairns to cover burial chambers and passageways. In the case of Newgrange, they faced the mound with white quartz – the same rock that was placed around the bones here. Under Ben Gorm, ancient people found a massive cap-stone ready-made.

These hunter-farmers of the Neolithic must have ranged widely over the uplands in their pursuit of game and pasture, but, like us, their lives were based in the shelter of lower areas along life-giving water bodies, grasslands and thickets. The uplands by contrast were territorial and ritual spaces. Studies of bone remains from other early burial sites, such as Aveline's Hole in the Mendip Hills of Somerset, suggest that the lives led by these early peoples were 'short and unthinkably hard', to use Robert Macfarlane's phrase.[25] Archaeological evidence from the Ben Gorm chamber gives us no clue to the origin or size of the community, nor to its relationship with other tomb-builders in the region. However, DNA analysis has shown links between the remains, suggesting that this was a small community using the site for grave rituals. All four main classes of megalithic tombs, court tombs, portal tombs, passage tombs, and wedge tombs are represented in Mayo, but the relationships and chronologies here are still debated. The court tomb is the most widely represented type in the region, with a dense distribution across north Mayo, Sligo and the north of Ireland, including two well-documented examples at Ballyglass and Behy in north Mayo. These tombs are contemporary with the grave rituals at Ben Gorm, but we have no idea how different groups interacted in the region at this time. Archaeologists are quick to point out that it took wealth, surplus and hierarchy to organise the construction of megalithic monuments, but none of that was needed for the rituals in the corrie above Lough Feeagh. We have no rock decorations, no grave artefacts, and – so far – no evidence of engineering, just the deposition of bones and a few quartz fragments. A small group could have achieved this, hiding their dead in the womb of the earth with a few gleams of quartz to light them through the darkness to the other world. For the living, this dry niche was a brief shelter from the hazards and insecurities of their world, where they ritualised the deaths, mostly of children, before returning to their swamps and drumlins.

For such weather-beaten, worn people, the climb from here to the top of Ben Gorm would have been a stroll, a few hours' detour to satisfy casual curiosity, or to see what fires were lit across the region. From the top of Ben Gorm, they could view the jagged arête slung between two peaks at the top of Glendahurk, or the summits of Nephin Beg and Corslieve to the north. At what point fires of ritual and sustenance became visible at the top of Corslieve we do not know, but at some stage in ancient times, a larger, more organised community went to the summit and constructed the huge cairn which we know nowadays as Leachta Dáithí Bán. This cairn, like Maeve's Cairn on Knocknarea, County Sligo, overlooks a landscape dotted with court tombs, and must conceal a grave chamber of some kind. At an altitude of 721 metres, the Corslieve cairn has a kind of lonely, forbidding eminence, marked in winter by sporadic coverings of snow, home of the white king, Dáithí Bán. Like any symbol of power and privilege, it has a magnetic force, and sits in my memory from the few trips I have made to the top. Sometimes, as I write, I feel drawn to the challenge of going there again, this time in winter, in the hope of putting boot prints across its snowy, unfrequented top in a gesture of pure expression. I also feel what Tim Robinson has referred to as 'the cumulative psychic presence' of these tombs, a 'massive' influence on him when he contemplated similar monuments in north-west Connemara. In a similar vein, Paul Evans celebrates such enquiry for its 'numinous moment of connection with the deep past which brings it into the present'.[26]

When I had left the chamber, Jessica noticed a butterfly flying around the main boulder. A peacock, it crossed and re-crossed the face of rock, exploring a few recesses as it moved. A symbol of the soul, of all souls that were remembered or forgotten in this place, it was an ephemeral sign of lightness, a brief material presence of something on its way. There could have been no greater contrast with the inert block of rock it flitted over.

The bowl of the corrie below the talus is well carpeted with heather and seemed almost cosy that afternoon: it would have made a sheltered spot for a picnic – midges permitting – but we wanted to investigate Lough Doo, the black lake, and so we continued along the rim of the moraine: the lake was a few hundred metres away, at a lower level, behind its own moraine to the south. By the time we got there, a breeze had picked up, funnelled across the side of a rocky ridge; the spot was cool, exposed, and bleak – unlike the sheltered bowl we had just left, so we hunkered down under a turf bank and ate a sandwich, giving up our thoughts of a wild swim in those dark waters.

As no homeward route across the bog is ever the same as the outward trek, our return took us closer to the edge of the trees. Instead of an upward slog across peat and pine roots, this was an easier stroll across lush molinia, deer sedge, beaked sedge, and mat grass, with the occasional bouquet of black bog rush. Deer sedge was already changing colour, giving an orange glow to the ground, and the stems of bog cotton were also turning a rich mahogany.

When we had come through a narrow section of plantation close to the car, the clearing was lit with peach-coloured spikes of bog asphodel, now gone to seed. The leaves were changing too into little crescents of a similar hue decorating the wet ground. Autumn, and the onset of winter, is this plant's best moment, when yellow flowers give way to a rich, flaring seed-head. As John F. Deane reminds us, in his beautiful meditation on western asphodels on Achill Island, 'Asphodel, according to the great stories of our mythology, is beloved of the dead and covers the plains of Hades. I came to have a vision of the surface of the bogs of Achill Island as imaging those rich and wind-blown plains of the afterworld.' The plant is sacred to Persephone, queen of the Underworld, who is imagined in classical mythology as deserting the fruitful earth during the winter, and spending the dark months with her husband Hades. She had been abducted by him, and would have been returned to the earth if she had not been tricked into eating pomegranate seeds from Hades' orchard. Having eaten food in the Underworld, she was confined there through the winter; but her origins as a vegetation goddess make Persephone also the bearer of new growth when she returns to the earth each spring, to be reunited with her mother Demeter, goddess of corn and crops.[27]

The Margins of Lough Feeagh

The day after the equinox, I set out early to look for a greenshank. The first storm of the year had scorched the trees and hedges, hastening the autumn. Ash was already lemon-yellow in places, with the keys, or seed bunches, darkening to chocolate-brown. Summer's ripeness was distilled to red points of fruit on rowan, holly and rose. Only grey willow, that hardy pioneer, still looked unchanged.

With a precious ridge of high pressure settled over Ireland, Lough Feeagh was very still: small rings of feeding trout stirred the surface, and a single herring gull sat like a buoy in the distance. Torc Shléibhe stood out from the grey hills in full light, like a round hat, green-yellow brimmed, chocolate-rust topped. A day like this allows the mind to focus and makes the present as stable and observable as memory.

When I was young, we would sometimes go as a family on winter afternoons to look at waders on the Shannon estuary at Ringmoylan. I saw my first greenshanks there, their pure white underparts conspicuous at a distance across the grey mudflats at low tide. They were also conspicuous as birds of less promising and more challenging places, such as muddy tidal creeks draining into the Shannon where you could not walk without being trapped by a deep, viscous silt that clung to your boots and kept your guilty, truant imprint. Several boyish excursions in those places were occasions of trespass and desolation, punctuated only by these unusual birds that would take off in terror at my approach.

Many years later, doing my bit for citizen science, I spent a day driving around the Mullet Peninsula counting greenshank in ones and twos along the shore. They seemed most at home there, a point of white purity in the endless skies and waters of north-west Erris. One bird I fixed on late in the day was busy in the shallows of an inlet near Glenamoy, fussing over something – a flatfish the size of a thumbprint, which it poked at and kept turning over in a dazzle of light from a low winter sun. The bird and its prey were an axis of life on which winter's elements turned, those vast waters and unendurable glare. By then I had read Desmond and Maimie Nethersole-Thompson's classic book on greenshanks, which gave a whole new dimension to this bird and described its other life on breeding grounds in northern Scotland.

Desmond Nethersole-Thompson was descended from an old school of egg-collectors and derived a lot of his knowledge of greenshank distribution in the nineteenth century from oologists who had gone to Scotland in search of this bird's eggs. His first study of greenshanks was in central Scotland, but in the 1960s he and his family began a fourteen-year campaign of fieldwork to study breeding greenshanks in north-western Scotland. The entire family of eight would go to Strath Dionard, a wild glen on the Gualin estate in Sutherland, where they lived in a small hut, enduring cramped conditions, exhaustion and the vicissitudes of Scottish weather for six weeks in May and June. Working as a team, including very young children, they amassed a huge body of data on the breeding behaviour of greenshanks and other waders: this work led to their monograph *Greenshanks* (1979), followed by another book on waders in 1986. In a nod to his earlier background as an egg-collector, Nethersole-Thompson wrote that 'For the nest hunter the greenshank has always been a blue riband bird.' The greenshank's elusiveness as a nester continued to obsess him throughout his long career as a field naturalist and led him and his family to find and document many nests on the stony flows. At times, the incubating birds eluded them for weeks: on their first season in the valley, the hunt for one of the nests started on 9th May, and was completed only on 27th, when he found a clutch just starting to hatch (his four-year-old son Patrick was with him on some of these forays).

In their fourth chapter on nest hunting, the authors describe the hunting method. The brooding bird on eggs sits very tight, and is so well camouflaged against the surrounding moss and stones that the observer can walk right past it. Brooding hens will even allow themselves to be stroked and touched. The partner is usually feeding at a body of water half a mile or more away. Twice a day the partners change over at the nest, so the nest hunter's tactic is to follow the relieving bird as it flies to the nest and its mate. 'We must now hold the rapidly flying bird in our binoculars and mark the furthest possible point along its flight line. The next day we start to watch there and hope to intercept the greenshank's flight.'[28]

By the time the authors settled down to write their preface, the family had found 300 greenshank nests and amassed a superb body of data on nesting biology. Tables and appendices in the monograph give details of occupied territories, breeding lives of females, population levels, continuity of nest sites, dates of laying, egg measurements, clutch sizes, incubation periods, chick measurements, and so on. A substantial fifth chapter on 'Voice' reproduces sonogram images of greenshank calls and songs, the result of much recording work on site by Desmond and the family, using equipment they had bought themselves. These are some of the scientific results which justified many years' labour and expense, tracking the authors' favourite bird, but beyond empirical methods and procedures, *Greenshanks* is also a family memoir of summers in northern Scotland, replete with paintings and drawings by their friend Donald Watson, and photographs by Eric Hosking and others. Given Desmond's authority and tenacity as a field ornithologist, the book comes laden with tributes from other collaborators and experts. There are other voices too, as sections of text reproduce short technical reports from other workers in the field, on diet, habitat and voice.

In a volume so freighted with diverse elements, you might think that its authorship would be dispersed, but as all components are directed towards the breeding biology of *Tringa nebularia*, this is not the case. Furthermore, although the book bristles with data, the passion of the scientist shines through the writing, and creates moments of intensity that we would normally associate with literary writing. 'Our greenshank valley,' the authors declare, 'is a land of changing colours. There are many evenings of incredible beauty. The river snakes and writhes with froth and creamy-coloured bubbles along its edge and on the pools. It disappears between brown banks, then foams relentlessly forward, rolling and pulsing towards the sea.'[29] In a heady section describing 'two beautiful greenshanks' mating, the cock's approach 'had beautiful grace', before 'the two beaks touched in a kiss and ... he dropped off her back.' The pair are last seen 'flashing over a ridge with their wild evocative cries soft in the wind.' Assenting to the moment, they write, 'the grace, movement and passion of this mating had created a poem of ecstasy and delight.'[30]

Touches of metaphor and figuration come through at other times. Referring to the birds of Scandinavian bogs, they write of 'the silvery tittering of whimbrels' among other bird sounds. When adult greenshanks call in alarm, 'their cries sound like tiny power-driven hammers beating small anvils.' The writing rises to the moment when an egg's colours are being described: they believe that the greenshank's eggs are the most beautiful of all British waders; one clutch 'was richly marked with red on a warm green ground with masses of underlying splashes of lavender and heliotrope.'

When I first read *Greenshanks*, the book gave me a scientific and literary portrait of what Donald Watson called flow country, that open, wet wilderness of blanket bog typical of much of northern Scotland. Mayo's greatest stretch of inland wilderness surrounding the Nephin Beg Mountains is such a habitat, although nowadays it has been substantially reduced by peat harvesting and forestry; a comparable expanse of flow country stretches from the coast between Clifden and Roundstone in Connemara to the Twelve Bens in the north. Many years ago, my brother Liam and I spent a long afternoon exploring one of the best stretches of flow country in Mayo, at Knockmoyle Nature Reserve near Bellacorick. The terrain seemed 'melancholy and featureless' (Derek Ratcliffe) at the outset, but as we walked into a vast space haunted by the plaintive calls of golden plover, a landscape gradually opened up with its own peculiar geography of locháns and small lakes. The monotony of brown bog gave way to a crazy paving of ponds and pools, the margins seamed with otter tracks. One of the largest locháns was several acres in extent, and as we approached its heathery edge we heard a big dog otter drop with a thud into the water. Although we watched the inert glitter for a long time there no sign of the creature. Our tally of bird species that day was a meagre eight, but it included dunlin, one of the few waders still breeding on those lonely bogs.

The habitat looked perfect for greenshanks, but we did not see any. If finding greenshank nests is a challenge for ornithologists in Scotland, then it is a vastly greater challenge in Ireland. In winter, greenshanks are widespread around Irish coasts, including Mayo, where they feed in sandy or muddy inlets very close to apparently suitable nesting habitat. The bulk of Irish wintering birds are from the Scottish breeding population, so it is intriguing that they are not tempted to nest on the Irish flows. There are, however, a tiny number of confirmed breeding records in Ireland, including two from Achill in the early seventies. Greenshanks have been rumoured to occur on Roundstone Bog in summer; and birds have been seen in recent years at a prime location in north Mayo, including a displaying pair in 2018. These records are largely stray observations by fieldworkers involved in other survey work, so it is tantalising to think what a dedicated effort at detection might reveal. Anyone who considers this challenge would do well to remember the Nethersole-Thompsons, who cautioned that they 'had lain up for many hours in early May, with little written in our notebooks at the end of each day... On many a day you never hear or see a greenshank; the egg lies wet and deserted in the scrape.' They should also bear in mind the misery inflicted by midges on outdoor activists in Mayo in summer, something the Nethersole-Thompsons were coy about mentioning.

Greenshanks become the character of winter around the margins of Lough Feeagh; they are absent in summer, having gone to their northern breeding grounds, but in winter they are thinly distributed around Irish and Scottish coasts where their high, nervy calls join with redshank and curlew in sandy and muddy inlets. In a few places, such as Lough Feeagh, they feed at the margins of fresh water.

Jessica and I had seen them regularly for a few years; during our walks the bird's calls would suddenly detonate from a shallow edge, and its long, rakish grey and white would arrow across the glare briefly before it settled. As bird sounds diminish during the winter, a greenshank's alarm becomes the essence of Lough Feeagh's black rocks and metallic water. They have a preference for the northern end of the lake, with its silted bays and shallows: they usually appear singly, their strident cries a clarion of solitude, but on one occasion Jessica and I flushed a group of three from the little bay cradled directly south of the promontory fort.

Today I was going to look for greenshanks where I had first encountered them, in the shallow bay at the mouth of the Glennamong River. I parked just before the fence barrier on the track running into Glennamong, and as I opened the car door a curlew called faintly somewhere in the distance, as if it yearned for recognition in this theatre of neglected presences. I was glad to be away again, firm-footed on a short moraine leading down to the shore. A slight breeze had picked up from the south; the water was like black silk being shaken gently. A small wave was dousing the tawny grain of a narrow beach in rapid beats.

The bay here is strewn with peat floes detached by erosion from the banks of the Glennamong River and pushed down into the lake by winter floods. A number of these fluvial erratics have sprouted willow trees during their long situation here; but a few smaller ones have in turn been pushed back ashore by southerly winds and dumped on the ground. I stopped on one of them to make notes – a raised, dry island of heather and asphodel surrounded by purple moor grass.

Then I continued, following the meanders of the Glennamong River upstream, its dark, soundless depths curving past levels of glacial sediment overlain with peat and skeletons of old pine. Like a giant black snake pushing to one side and then the other as it moves, this river is constantly wearing away its margins. At several turns, huge peat floes were collapsing from the bank, revealing a darkness of millennia, thousands of years of depositions, sedimentation and peat growth undermined by winter floods. These sections were as fresh as meat cut open by a cleaver; one big, recent break in a root stump was as bright as butter.

Eventually, the deep, slack pools gave way to gravelly shallows which I could wade across, allowing me to turn back towards the lake again. There is one magnificent ox-bow on this far side, a section of old river abandoned decades ago when floods broke through into a new channel. It is now festooned with sedge and water lilies but still has enough open water to hold a pair of mallard – they exploded from the margin when I approached, the air whetting the rapid beat of their wings.

As I continued my search of the little pools and inlets of the bay, I wanted the day to be defined by the sudden call of indignation when the lanky, grey-and-white agitation of a greenshank fled in outrage at my presence. But it never happened. The stillness was an unveiling of meadow pipit and wren calls, and a few notes from a stonechat. Apart from a few honks from Glennamong's passing ravens, the rest was silence. Swallows had deserted these upland glens, and the common sandpiper, another wader that enlivens these lonely bodies of fresh water throughout the summer, was on its way back to the coast of West Africa. On another occasion, I had risen greenshank, common snipe and jack snipe in this spot, but now there was not a single wader, except for the curlew heard at the start, a plaintive sentry for all these creatures under threat everywhere and now in decline. The call of the greenshank, and its white agitation in the darkness of these bays, was a thing withheld by the narrowing year. I would go again in search of it, or be surprised by its unexpected appearance in a different place.

Like a curtain being lifted on the morning, the drone of an outboard engine came across the water: an angling boat appeared, with two anglers and their gillie. I was now observed rather than observer, a blue mark two hundred metres away. The boat patrolled the shallow waters of the bay for a short while and then settled beyond a bank of emergent vegetation. The two fishermen flicked their lines onto a stretch of calm water where trout were rising; a message alert sounded on a mobile phone.

Their presence roused me into activity. Some impulse of self-awareness prompted me to look busy, as if I were a research scientist studying vegetation or soil. There seemed to be no prospect of greenshanks, so I looked again, as if with professional purpose, at plants that had drawn my amateur curiosity: black bog rush, purple moor grass, heath rush, deer sedge, beaked sedge, mat grass and cotton grass. The purple moor grass, deer sedge and cotton grass were showing a blend of rust and yellow, a blush that would change whole landscapes as winter approached. In one damp flush, a large patch of bog cotton had turned a deep saffron colour, and contrasted beautifully with stands of bleached-out rushes.

Lacking the technicalities of botany, I have developed my own figurations of these plants to add to various hints and insights given by colleagues and friends: black bog rush with its dark lance-heads; the deep, sibilant tussocks of purple moor grass and its dry-spaghetti flowering stalks; tight, shiny basal clusters of heath rush; punk-peroxide tufts of mat grass with stray blonde stalks; horse-mane hairs of deer sedge, the stems turning stripy yellow, then black in gradual bands; seed heads of beaked sedge held on separate stems, like lamp-stands; cotton grass flaring deep green or mahogany off bare peat. Along with heathers and mosses, these plants are the walker's constant companion on the bogs and uplands; even where they have been cropped and trampled by hungry sheep, and thus make their way into public controversy as evidence of degradation, each of them has their character nonetheless and they make a continual running show as the walker judges the ground for each step in turn. I respect them all as tokens of resilience on ground that lacks nearly everything a creature might require in terms of sustenance: they seem to need only rainwater to give colour and texture to winter walks in the hills, before they surrender to the peat that originally brought them into the world.

I prodded at a few clumps of sedge and removed some stalks to take with me for later examination with a hand lens. Then it was time for me to go, leaving the anglers in the desertion of the bay. As I approached the car, a kestrel flew across, and hoisted itself onto an invisible ledge in the air; it hovered in a fixed position, with the vigorous motion of wings keeping its body and eyes poised over the ground. A pair of hoodies drifted across and nudged it away casually: the kestrel flew on towards Glennamong.

That day, like many others, was infused by the absence of the thing I had hoped to see. Scarcity or rarity are qualities that always sharpen the watcher's appetite, but too often these are part of a process of species decline and habitat loss, and it is hard to shake off a melancholy from this knowledge. On the other hand, there are creatures to be encountered if we have the patience to look for them, where their absence reflects our lack of attention and the impatient rhythm of our crowded lives. There is enough evidence now to hint at greenshanks breeding in north Mayo: they are there, for those who are determined to find them.

From Treanlaur to Derrybrock

The Western Way runs through the townland of Treanlaur (An Trian Láir, the middle third) along an old glacial moraine, one of a parallel series lying in a north-south axis through Srahmore. There's another, higher track, parallel to the Western Way, which is easily reached if you park at the new gateway and stile; instead of entering the Western Way, you stay on the tarred road, and walk uphill until it turns right, heading south. Just after the turn, a grassy ramp on your left leads to the start of the upper track: a loosely secured fence opening is the walker's portal to another time.

The track is still in good condition, a sheltered stony way between lines of grey willow and holly; tractors and quad bikes can travel here, successors to the ponies and traps, donkeys and carts of an earlier age.

As I walked here one morning in mid-October, meadow pipits were sipping at a silence and a few mistle thrushes were rattling in a belt of conifers. I stood in the shade of these trees and saw sunlight at a low angle spilling into the space of a derelict field. The tussocks were golden in that light; the space was fractured by strands of gossamer as fine as cracks in glass, as spiderlings took a lift of air to their new lives. My binoculars found these long, hairline glitters flashing as the gossamer tilted in the sunlight, with each spiderling suspended as a tiny white mote among drifts of flies.

As I went on, leaving the conifers behind, the track became more open and prone to exposure. Well-spaced hawthorns on either side struck their attitudes of torment, a constant reminder that benign weather was a luxury in this exposed place.

By now a derelict house known locally as Sheehan's was visible a couple of hundred metres ahead: a south-facing, two-storey farmhouse mantled with mature sycamores. The Sheehans were land stewards for Captain Charles Laprimandage, a French officer who had befriended the Marquis of Sligo during the Crimean War in the 1850s and received from him a large tenancy around Lough Feeagh.[31] The house in its bleak isolation is a memorial to Victorian progress, a spirit which reached far into this part of Mayo in the nineteenth century. Looking across at this land from the top of Crimlin, the farm appears as a long, narrow patchwork of fields surrounded by blanket bog. In bright October sunlight, this green strip turns golden, as these labour-intensive lands were now reclaimed by moor grass.

The late nineteenth century house might not have any neo-Georgian pretensions; its design is plain and unadorned, but its aspect and position proclaim a new relationship with the landscape: to view and be viewed. It did this defiantly, putting no obstacle between its broad façade and the prevailing wind; it boasts a wide optical empire stretching to Ben Gorm and the arête at Glendahurk in the west, and southwards across the islands of Clew Bay as far as Croagh Patrick. All the venerable sycamores planted here are clustered to the sides and at the back, but by a wild irony, one tree has seeded naturally and flourishes above the front porch; its roots have fingered under the plasterwork and now grip the stonework in a monstrous embrace. Another feral tree sits on the wall of the rear scullery amid decorations of spleenwort and dandelion.

The narrow porch, which is entered from the side, shields the front door from the elements; in the centre it has a small window framing a view of Clew Bay and the Reek. Once in through the front door, you stand in what used to be the central hallway, now a grassy floor marked by a badger's probings. To the left is the parlour, with another, larger window commanding the perspective to Clew Bay; the kitchen is on the right, with an iron stove and fireplace still intact, sinking into a residue of ash and soot. I stooped under the huge lintel stone breasting the chimney and stared up into the corbelled chimney tapering away into the darkness.

With their original mortar crumbled away, the walls here rise all the way to the apex of the roof about twenty-two feet higher. With the first floor rotted out, leaving only the joist sockets, the eye can admire the entire stretch of stonework, a tightly constructed smooth mosaic of local geology, grey quartzite, greenish schists, bone-coloured quartz, and red sandstone. The cornerstones visible on the outside are from local sandstone, a rock that occurs naturally in mason-friendly blocks and was used here to set the corners of the house.

On my October visit, the house was a gallery of light and shadow, with views of the landscape suspended at different levels in the window openings. The house is still a home for ghosts of the busy people here who kept fires lit, did household chores, read newspapers, managed the complex life of the farm, and hoped that their spirit of enterprise could hold out against the severe challenges of weather in Burrishoole. I noticed that one upstairs bedroom window, designed to look out on Ben Gorm and the peaks of Glendahurk, had been built in, having evidently been defeated by the nagging vandalism of winter storms. On a day like this, however, the house's setting was at its best: fully open to daylight from mid-morning, the sun slowly directing its theatre of sky and mountain until it finally disappeared shortly before sunset behind the ridges of

Glennamong. The south-facing windows of the kitchen, parlour and both upstairs bedrooms were all votaries of this light: the domestic industries of scullery, henhouse and outhouse were clustered at the back, in a twilight under sycamores, serving this devotion to Apollo.

I sat for a while outside on a grassy bank in the sun, looking up through the branches of mature trees, marvelling at their lichens, thinking of chaffinch and goldfinch nests neatly shielded with this material as camouflage. Then I stepped over a modern sheep fence, crossed the little stream with its constant traffic of water sounds, and picked my way among the enclosures in the shadow of the house. Some of this stonework, built by less specialised hands, is crumbling away, and another invasive sycamore has rooted above the ruins, like the pine trees that grew above derelict Neolithic walls at Céide. But once you leave the deep gloom of these trees, there are many other exposed stones about the size of basketballs which are covered in a brilliant emulsion of white lichen; at the edge of this open area an old herdsman's cottage, which predates the main house, sits with its back to the track and preserves its own humble record of collapse and partial repair.

There's one more boundary stream to cross: it defines another grassy, well-drained field, with a curious set of stone clusters. Each of these, about three feet by eight, is a set of rocks – I'm tempted to say megaliths – roughly poised and tilted together as if the farm had its own cemetery of wedge tombs. I leave their obscure legacy to some future archaeological survey of this site.

Leaving this field was an easy step over a sheep fence and a boundary wall onto the continuation of the track. The track is now somewhat rougher, a double spoor kept open by tractor and quad tyres through a thick growth of rushes.

The civilising legacy of Sheehan's farm is still visible on the left in the handsome walls enclosing the last fields of the holding. As this land is spared the worst pressures of commonage grazing, molinia and other moorland grasses have proliferated, and with them the insect-eating birds that spend the winter here. Meadow pipits, stonechats, wrens and reed buntings were escorts and adornments along walls and fences; and the little wren even managed a few bursts of song to celebrate the pleasures of the day.

The track is now a dual seam in the overgrazed desolation of the bog. Just a few hawthorns and rowans memorialise the destruction of woodland vegetation across this open area: there is little for the eye to focus on in these featureless undulations, at first glance at least. That is, until memory and folklore, led by some innocent exploration, bring their scrutiny to bear on the next townland, Derrybrock.

I followed the track dutifully for a kilometre past Sheehan's until the first glitter of Derrybrock Lough appeared on the bog. The name Doire Bhroc, badger wood, was another reminder of the desertification of this landscape; I wanted to revisit this obscure football pitch of silver and its eponymous townland for another reason. The area has an old association with fairies, a place where children were warned never to go. A recent map marks a tree to the west of the lake as a fairy tree, crann na sí, which was probably the catalyst for my strange bewilderment on an earlier visit, when I thought I had divined an aspect of the area's 'psychic memory', to use a phrase from Synge.

Jessica and I had come along the Western Way, past the newly updated section, and had crossed a bluff above the track with the forlorn remains of a cottage and cultivation ridges. We stopped briefly at the lake, and then turned back towards the little sheltered glen between the lake and the Western Way. I was drawn to a group of old hawthorns in a coombe separated from the Way by a low ridge. A stonechat flew up from one of the hawthorns and vanished. When I had finished nosing around and writing a few notes, I went to rejoin Jessica, thinking that she must be just around the corner, in the little gully taking the stream down to the main track. But there was no sign of her. When I stepped over the low ridge to get a view of the track, I still couldn't see her; then I thought she might have fallen into the narrow gully at the stream and searched urgently for a few moments. With no sign of her there either, in mounting anxiety, I imagined she might have misread the waymarked posts and gone down towards the peat workings at the base of Crimlin – but she had disappeared.

I was completely spooked by now: the terrain had seemed open to my view: a few ridges and hollows between a lake and a track just a few hundred metres apart, a delay of a couple of minutes while I looked around and scribbled some notes, and my wife had vanished. I felt that the place was haunted by a sinister force; I shouted several times, to no avail. My confidence in my own experience, in my 'feel' for these remote places, was gone. As a last resort, I continued along the way, wondering whether some petulance had impelled her forward, and a couple of minutes later she appeared on the brow of a slope above the trail about two hundred metres away. She waved to me, and I waved back.

When I got to her, we blustered through explanations; I checked the map and again saw the name 'crann na sí', which I had spotted earlier and not paid much heed to. On that occasion, nothing seemed to make sense, apart from a visitation of an occult influence – not my own tardiness, not Jessica's hurrying on, not a trivial but still disturbing break in communication. The stonechat's flight was terror-struck, as if it confirmed the foreboding. We continued our talk about psychic influences on our way back to the road among deep stands of rhododendron.

At any rate, that moment at Derrybrock had fixed the place in our memories, like a peg on a steep face to support a step or a story; but my mood had changed, the influence of the little people had receded, when I went back to Derrybrock a few weeks later and walked past Sheehan's onto the wide tract of open ground. Birreencorragh was just visible behind Mount Eagle with a white cap of snow. A few unfamiliar bird calls broke the January stillness, and I tracked a small, tantalising flock across the stony flanks of Buckoogh for a while, but could not get a proper view. (My trawl of the sound archive that evening discovered that they were siskins, a common species of forestry plantations.)

Then I turned west past the lake and approached the hollow with the fairy trees. I noticed a fox moving across the bottom; it had not seen me, so I crouched down to watch it with binoculars. It paused occasionally to pounce on small prey in the tussocks, sticking its snout into the growth; it was engrossed in this hunt and showed no caution about anyone nearby. The animal's movement across the hollow brought it towards me and eventually it came to within forty metres. A low afternoon sun meant that I was dissolved in glare from the animal's point of view; and the animal itself was lit perfectly. The white fur on its chin and throat was as pure as the icing on a Christmas cake; the rust on its head and snout were orange with brightness, the legs and back darker, the flanks the colour of estuary mud.

I make a brief 'chak' noise, like the note of a stonechat; then another, and this time the fox looks up briefly. It doesn't see anything, the little noise has no meaning for it and so it resumes its hunt in the tussocks. I'm trying to communicate with this fox, to have some exchange that will not disturb it from its vivid innocence, and to do this I must stay crouched down, hiding my real identity. I make the little noise again, like a bird note that cannot signify 'food'; the fox looks up and stares directly towards me: I have fox-eye in my binoculars, still oblivious to me as a human. Once more it turns away, and I tempt it a final time with a little noise; again I have fox iris looking in my direction, empty of the recognition that is about to erupt. I stand up gradually, taking human shape against the sun – the fox is suddenly electrified with terror. It turns, scuttling off across the bog, gaining ground and speed, as if its fox brain were accelerating on the dawning realisation of its misjudgement of those little calls it heard and did not recognise. I lost the fox among the gentle undulations of the moor, and continued on, full of guilty satisfaction.

On my first visit to Derrybrock I had been wrong-footed by a fairy tree; on the second it was a fox whom I had taunted with deception; on the third, I set out with cold curiosity to see if there was anything else I could add to my sense of this proscribed zone.

This time, I approached the lake reverentially, crossing a flat expanse of deer sedge and mat grass descending into a boggy hollow just south of it. A few thin ribbons of aquatic weed were spread across the surface, and other plant stalks with flosses of algae receded into the tea-coloured depths. An abandoned water tank sitting in a couple of feet of water at the northern end held my attention, but as I marched towards it, I spotted a cluster of quartz stones set on the grassy top of a peat bank at the water's edge. The largest stone was as big as a cow's head, the smallest fist-sized.

They were sunk in the grassy sward and had not been shifted for years. I had seen such clusters before, on the Bangor Trail, wayside cairns marking a spot where someone had died, and I thought that these stones marked a death, perhaps a drowning or suicide at the secluded lake. (Others will say that this is the site of a cillín, or children's burial place.) This thought took the mystery away from the putative association with fairies and gave the place a different, secular sense as a spot where a life had ended, and where others had put quartz stones on a bank as a memorial. While I believed I knew why children were warned to stay away from this place, when I sat down nearby, taking a reflective break, a gust of wind through rushes made me start, as though I were still prone to superstitious visitations.

The outflow from the lake ran through a swamp of sphagnum and rushes into a smaller pond, tennis-court size, with a fading crop of water lilies. The flowering stalks sticking out of the water were spent at the ends, like extinguished matches. This pond, in turn, delivered water into a little stream among rushes that cut a channel into the drift and spread out into the damp flush where I had met my fox. Four mallard took off from this wet ground when I appeared and turned overhead, a smart squadron in fly-past. This squashy glen, with its relict fairy thorns, sits in an armchair of bluffs and hillocks formed by glacial drift: the highest point overlooking the trees is known as Cnoc na Sí or Pull Hill. Pull or poll is a nearby depression, which has again been promoted to the height, giving the oxymoronic name. Nosing around the top, I heard a few distant notes from a refugee curlew; there were old trenches where the peat layer had been cut out for fuel, and in the grassy areas, dense punctuations of psilocybin mushrooms: these magic hallucinogens could be the occasion for another mode of derangement or haunting.

Having established so many paths to bewilderment in my own mind, I looked with a secular eye at the hawthorns, a stand of very old trees rotting away under a hoar burden of *Cladonia* and *Evernia* lichens, with a whitewash of *Schizopora* fungus on the main branches. Two old hoodie nests were visible in the tops, one holding a flourish of weedy growth like a hanging basket. Unplugged from old associations, the hawthorns stand as survivors in a landscape 'sheepwrecked', to use George Monbiot's phrase.

Before I came off the ridge, I heard shouts from the lower track and saw a sheepman's dog run into the narrow glen below me, heading for a small flock of sheep in the hollow. The man then appeared for a moment on the ridge line close to me and shouted again at the dog, calling it back. The dog returned to its owner, and they both went back down to the track. Neither of them had any inkling that I was present looking down at them. One's own unobserved presence on a hillside has something weird about it, something *unheimlich* in these contested territories of the western uplands. This informs my own sense that you can never trust your solitude in what passes for wilderness and you should always assume that the hills are watching.

EAST

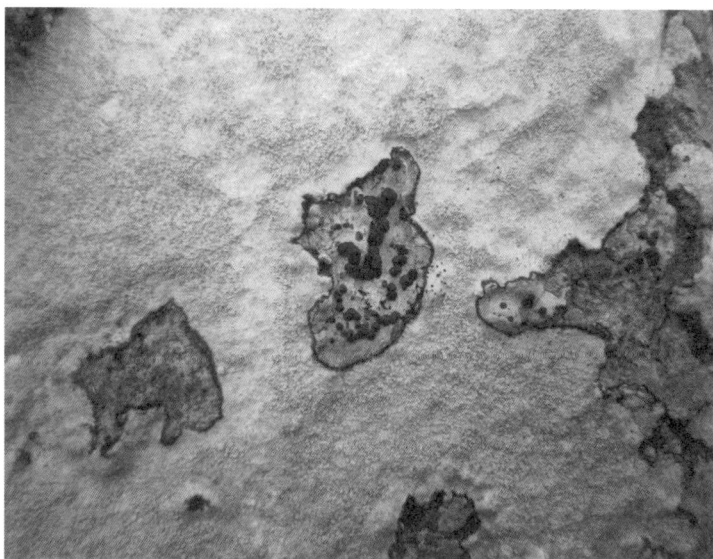

Glenlara

While mountains might be supposed to be fixed and stable as components of a landscape, in reality they are very versatile and their appearance is subject to many variables. Changes in atmospheric pressure as well as weather cause mountains to slip into and out of focus, to be magnified or to diminish at a distant remove. Much more understandably, though still remarkably, mountains rearrange themselves in a landscape as a walker moves through it; a walker can move mountains, turning them round as he or she moves round them.

I notice this as I drive from Westport to my house five kilometres away to the north-east. As the road swings, dips and rises among the drumlins, there's a constant variation in the horizon to the north: at first it is the distant pyramid of Nephin which engages the eye in the distance; then the road aims towards the smooth brow of Buckoogh; later still, another series of peaks comes into view between Mount Eagle and the summit of Birreencorragh. When Mount Eagle gets focussed by the lens of atmospheric pressure, it appears much closer than its normal remoteness partly dissolved in mist. On this flattened, two-dimensional canvas, Mount Eagle belies its position at the upper end of a narrow glen; and if we had no other reason for going there, history alone might be enough to lead us in.

The glen Mount Eagle overlooks is a narrow, forested pass between Buckoogh to the west and the flank of Birreencorragh to the east. The glen itself is called Glenlara (Gleann Lára, valley of the mare); but the area is also known as Skerdagh, from its rocky, tumbling river, an scoirdach. Whereas the main pedestrian route through the Nephins leads past Loughs Furnace and Feeagh on the other side of Buckoogh, the pass at Skerdagh offers an alternative, one that appealed to rebels on a number of occasions in the past. Glenlara is fixed in local memory as the place where the Newport curate Fr Manus Sweeney first went into hiding during the 1798 Rebellion. He spent seven weeks there in the house of Thady Moran and his wife Brigid McFadden before moving to Camcloon, near Newport, where he hid for another six weeks in a concealed shelter under a turf stack. Father Sweeney was eventually arrested on Achill and subsequently sentenced to death for his part in the rebellion. His public hanging in Newport on 8th June 1799 is still vividly remembered in the Nephins as a defining incident of the Year of the French.[32]

During the War of Independence, Skerdagh was the scene of a deadly encounter on 23rd May 1921, a few days after the Kilmeena ambush, when an IRA brigade lay in wait for a police and army patrol on its way out of Westport and came off worst when the firing started. Four IRA Volunteers and an RIC officer were killed at Kilmeena, and several Volunteers were wounded and captured. The IRA brigade retreated to Skerdagh, where they went to ground until the police and army noose tightened in on them: on 23rd May, another gunfight took place in the glen, with two more fatal casualties, one on each side. Eventually, the leaders of this brigade under the command of Michael Kilroy crept past the police cordon at night and escaped to the south; the rest of the column, including two wounded, were guided over the hills towards Leana and Bunaveela where they found food and shelter. The wounded men, disguised as women, were smuggled out through Glendavollagh, while the remainder of the column, numbering about twenty, continued over the passes into Glendahurk, to another safe house.

While the detail of cross-dressing IRA men gives the story a certain contemporary appeal, my main satisfaction here comes from the account of a rebel trail running across the mountains at an angle to the tourist-approved Bangor Trail and Western Way. Along the way this route revives and keeps open at least two instances of the term mám, the Irish for pass: one taking the rebels into Glennamong, and the other, Mám a' Chaorthainn, allowing them into Glendahurk to the west. These placenames, with their suggestions of country people moving about their business across these hills, have been stored in the memory of a very few hill farmers, although they are being revived nowadays by map-savvy hill walkers.

I went to Skerdagh to explore this trail for myself one morning in late November. The weather had been dominated by cold easterlies for a few days, pitching us into winter; the last leaf-show of autumn was the fall of orange ovals from grey willow, a steady grain letting go in the early silence. As I drove into the valley from Glenhest, the two pillars of the glen, Buckoogh and Birreencorragh, were hidden in cloud, while the southern horizon behind me was a smouldering blur of apricot under a lid of showers.

My tentative plan was to climb Mount Eagle and inspect the mám to the right, which led down into forestry on the other side; this was in preparation for a longer day's walking as far as a cave at Correenmore where IRA Volunteers rested before continuing on to Glendahurk. But my interest in the Skerdagh valley had another strand: there were old references to eagles in the area, in Glenlara and on Buckoogh. An old reference to golden eagles on Buckoogh had always intrigued me, and I wondered if the cliff above Loch na mBreac Caoch, the lake of the one-eyed trout, could have hosted an eyrie. I wanted to investigate this corrie under Buckoogh before attempting Mount Eagle, and so, the historian in me giving way to the amateur ornithologist, I decided to make for the eastern slope of Buckoogh, Taobh a' Locháin, which would get me to the lake.

The inner part of Glenlara is a narrow valley, with stands of conifers and some broadleaves in various stages of growth. Forestry roads make most of it accessible nowadays so I drove past a few old memorials: a windowless house with lozenge-shaped patterns of seashells, and a ruined stone cottage where a surf of golden fuchsia washed over the walls. When I parked at the forest edge, a short walk through high spruce got me onto the open hillside.

A few calling hoodies were the first breaches in the morning silence: I was climbing gradually, at a steady, lazy pace, following a line parallel to a long strip of conifers which ended close to the rim of the corrie. Then a large bird appeared from another mature spruce plantation over to the north where it may have roosted: I first thought 'buzzard', but as it flew in my direction the wings were too long, so I calculated 'harrier', until I realised that this bird was much bigger. Then the pale tail and primaries came into focus and I realised that it was a juvenile golden eagle. It crossed the hillside and disappeared above another section of plantation; a moment later it flew up again and was briefly mobbed by two hoodies, and then I caught a glimpse of it at the top of the plantation, where the trees ended just under the corrie. I thought that would be my lot for the day and climbed on towards the lake. The corrie itself was clouded in, but as I came level with the top of the plantation, a silhouette materialised out of the mist above me, and then glided lower, emerging into the light – it was my eagle, gliding rapidly lower, stooping twice towards a kestrel pair quartering the sky above a clearing. The kestrels looked diminutive, swift-sized, beside this monarch of the glen. Before I realised what these falcons were, I cheered on the eagle, 'Come on, teach them who's boss,' as if it was putting manners on a pair of upstart hoodies. I wanted the eagle to have ownership of the valley.

I had the eagle fixed in my binoculars as it turned without a wingbeat and took a lift from the wind up the glen; after a few moments it came back, sliding on the pressure of a breeze blowing against it; I followed it carefully as it sailed out towards Glenhest and then, on purposeful wingbeats, headed off. A coastguard helicopter made noise overhead at that moment, and the wind turbines at Croaghmoyle framed its horizon as it faded away.

This was my first sighting of a golden eagle in Mayo. I had followed the fortunes of Ireland's eagles ever since the first eagle reintroduction programme from 2000 and had been hoping to see both golden and sea eagles back in Mayo skies, returning to the wild places where they had lived until their extermination in the early twentieth century. Golden eagles were now established in Donegal, with a handful of pairs breeding in the mountains; I had heard of a few sightings in the Sligo Leitrim uplands, but very few had made it as far as Mayo. This bird had probably fledged from a nest in Donegal in 2017, to judge from the stage of its plumage. Sea eagles from the second Irish reintroduction programme in Kerry had begun to turn up in the south of the county, around Killary Harbour and Lough Mask, but a golden eagle was unexpected and I counted this sighting as an even greater prize. The bird I had watched above the conifers was, in a sense, returning to this valley; golden eagles were known to occur there until the early twentieth century, and they had given their name to the hill overlooking the glen.

My sighting was a homecoming, a restoration; my sense of the place was deeply enhanced – I whooped and punched the air. An eagle in Glenlara! Yes!

I had a new motivation to continue climbing to the lake of the one-eyed trout. There was an old reference to golden eagles on Buckoogh and I wondered if the cliffs above the lake were high enough to hold an eyrie. I reached the rim of the corrie and tramped across green-golden sphagnum to the lake, a shallow pitch of water choked with spear-blade leaves of *Potamogeton*. The next plantation to the north presented a wall of big spruce blocking the hillside. It was at first difficult to examine the corrie wall: veils of cloud were sweeping through; then came a brightening, the sun's disc was there, moderated like a full moon. Then the veil's hem rose, as if a great celebrity were lifting her cloak, the sun's spotlight ready, the corrie a stage about to be lit – but the veil came down again, tantalisingly; sunlight was a straggling gleam to the south, the corrie was in cloud and shadow.

When the vapour thinned once more, rocks were visible overlooking the lake: a ten-minute scramble took me up to the most promising site, like a fortified bastion twenty feet high, with a sheltered ledge and a sheer face underneath. This was inaccessible to fox or man and I noted it as a possible eyrie site. Mount Eagle itself had presented a similar challenge: despite the name, there was no cliff that seemed high or secure enough to hold breeding eagles, so I have come to think of it as a soaring, preening and gathering site, rather than one that ever hosted breeding birds. From the side of Buckoogh where I stood it was a short glide across the valley to Mount Eagle, a hill at the head of the valley well supplied with funnelling winds to lift soaring, hunting eagles.

My route back down took me along the upper edge of a big spruce plantation. The fenced-off ground within the plantation was deeply carpeted with wood rush, a plant I had not seen in such profusion on flat terrain previously. This rush is a favourite material used by golden eagles in Scotland to line their nests, so the plant had a different appearance and meaning here, as part of my eagle ecology.

When I rounded the plantation and turned downhill, I had to struggle through a young spruce plantation, six or seven years old, an area that had previously been clear-felled and was a mass of old brash and forty-year-old stumps. It was desperate going, but I was cheered by many signs of red deer: branch damage, browsing, tracks and droppings. I stumbled and staggered along in the knowledge that this place offered few openings for the hunter and that the deer were secure. The peaty bank that finally led onto the track after half a kilometre's toil was trampled and slotted by deer prints.

When you get off the slopes and open ground, there's a feeling of security in conifer plantations, despite the bad reputation they have among ecologists. A sky of wind became a susurration of spruce needles at a high remove from where I stood, shielded from the empire of the elements. Sunlit banks along the track showed a flourishing of ling (*Calluna*), bell heather, and cross-leaved heath; grey willow along the edge was heavily browsed; sphagnum was a soft paradise of neon green in the ditches. Then a female sparrowhawk took off from a mixed woodland fringe and flashed away over the treetops, a sign that there was enough life here to feed her.

The entire length of track I walked on my way back to the car was a woodland ride densely marked by browsing deer.

Three days later, in the same place, Jessica and I were gifted with a sighting we had not expected. Walking up the valley along the forestry track, a hind appeared a hundred metres ahead, grazing an open area at a fork in the track. A low sun behind us meant that we were lost in glare from the animal's point of view, exactly the same conditions as those that got me so close to the fox at Derrybrock. We watched the warm brown and beige of the animal's hindquarters for a minute; then an antlered stag stepped onto the track, and two more young bucks followed. Despite Jessica's pink jacket, they had no inkling of our presence. The two youngsters squared up to each other and clashed antlers a few times, imitating the fierce contests they must have witnessed during the recent rut. We were enthralled by this piece of real-life footage and out of reverence turned away from the track and walked off to the river without disturbing them.

Twenty minutes later we came back, expecting them to have vanished, but as we came on, the older stag and a young buck were still there in the clearing: we got to within twenty metres before they ran off into the forest: their antlers clashed like knitting needles against low branches. Later during our walk, a deer's braying echoed up to the high track from the bottom of the glen, a mixed thicket of willow, young spruce, and birch.

All this sense of life gave buoyancy to our step as we continued up the glen to the very end of the track. The Buckoogh side where we walked was mostly in shadow. The far side of Glenlara, a western spur off Birreencorragh, was lit intermittently by the sun; beyond that, higher up, the summit showed now and then, with the point of its cairn a marker for distance, elevation, and a measure of awe. The lower flank of the mountain kept the eye entertained: moving cloud made large intrusions of colour and light; ground shared a sense of movement, which was not the preserve of sky and cloud only, but the hillside moved in colour with the moving light, and as we walked up the glen, the mountain to our right was shifting, slipping back down the valley as we made progress, a peak that had been remote, awkward, unreachable, had now been tamed by the distance we had come and now lay directly beside us, within our compass.

Spurred by my recent sighting, the following day I was determined finally to go to the top of Mount Eagle, hoping that the eagle might still be in the valley. I parked at the ford and walked along the overgrown margins of the winding river until I got out onto open ground. Forestry plantation comes right down to the river's edge on the western side of the glen; the eastern side is open hillside. The main feature here is a series of deep creases formed by streams running off the mountain. The map marks this flank of the mountain as Meall Mór, which suggests a fleshy protuberance, and there is now a fitting, exposed nudity in the yellow-green hillside where all the heather cover has been grazed away.

I trudged towards a stone cottage at the very top of the catchment, just at the base of Mount Eagle. It is known locally as Mrs Dyra's. As I made my way along the wet bottom of the slope, I came across an old sheep carcass, now reduced to a bundle of rib bones like an antique tribal necklace at the collar of a long train of blackening fleece. It had been many months since ravens, hoodies and the fox quarrelled over this carrion – could this have been the sheep that was breathing its last as I passed by here four years earlier on my first eagle searches?

Then the first field boundaries of an old farming settlement began to appear. These are now stone-faced clay banks or levees emerging from the rushes, enclosing former meadows, pastures and crop fields. As I approached the cottage there were more of them on either side of a cheerful, rocky stream that gathered all the water from the higher slope of Meall Mór. The levees held a line on either side of the tributary stream, several feet above the river level; these mountain streams can rise with devastating power during periods of heavy rain. Such streams in north Mayo deposit silt and gravel along their margins, creating better-drained ground; but the same power can wreck meadow grass and vegetable crops along the floodings.

It was partly this effect of rivers which allowed people to settle in these remote river valleys in the past. Cattle found sweet pickings along the grassy margins of spate rivers; river gravels could be mixed with peaty soil to improve drainage in crop fields, and even to raise ground levels away from floods. Levees were built of clay and stone to defend the fields from rising levels, and in this way little meadows could be protected, allowing cattle to be overwintered on sites that previously were summer pastures only.

As I pottered about taking photographs of the farming site under Mount Eagle, I was vividly aware of the labour that went into farming in these remote places; all that effort memorialised now in stone walls, cottages, booley huts and levees within the silence of the moor. A tiny jetty at a fording place on the stream formed a trough of deeper water where clothes must have been washed as the laughter and gossip of women animated this space above the lambency of running water. Fifty metres higher up, the walls of a small outhouse have been adapted and extended to form a handling pen for sheep, the crushed rushes and abandoned plastic bottles a sign that this place is still occasionally visited by working life. On the other side of the stream was a beautifully preserved booley hut: the clay walls were now mossed over and rushes flourished in the enclosed space, but this hut was protected by a second wall like a shield; all it needed was a roof of branches and scraws to make a summer bivvy. Whoever stayed up here with the cattle in the summer had their dreams visited by the sound of running water.

The main stone cottage is a handsome structure of tight stonework, most of it schist set neatly in mortar. As well as the fireplace you would expect to find in the main room, the bedroom also had its own fire, a concession to modern comfort. Using an unlettered rule of thumb and eye, I thought this house, with its nod to improved standards of living, was a product of the post-Famine era. Someone made a pitch at living here all year round on the site of an old booley and set a Victorian spirit of determination and progress against the old ways of husbandry and weather. How long that experiment held out in the teeth of Glenlara's winters was a secret I could not extract from the collapsed stones and the litter of fleece in the main room.

It was midday, and I had to suspend my musings on this piece of bygone real estate in order to climb to the top. Stepping up the slope, I recited an internal mantra of plants I could identify on the depleted ground: heath rush, mat grass, sphagnum, all that was left after decades of grazing pressure. Then, at nearly 400 metres, a deeper *Racomitrium* moss of the uplands, spread in soft tussocks all across the hilltop. I picked a small piece of quartz and added it to the modest cairn.

The name Mount Eagle appears to be a late addition to this hill, known traditionally as Sceilpín, little crag, from the steep flanges of bare rock on the northern side. I scrambled about on these to check for eagle-friendly ledges but saw nothing that was steep enough. From here I had a view of conifers flooding the glen below like a tsunami, and a series of peaks and ridges ending at Corslieve over thirteen kilometres away. The nearest hill was Gogín (possibly from goigín, a small heap), a northward extension of the hilltop I was standing on; its plump, swollen summit was another meall mór, a fleshy protuberance. All of these were free of cloud except Corslieve, which wore a swirl of white like a badge of privilege.

In the biting wind of late November, the heights were no place to linger – and I was oppressed by this open, barren hillside. To give me another interest on my way down, I headed back towards the slope of Meall Mór and the main gully of the tributary streams. One silver rowan rising out of the throat of this gully gave me hopes of something more: the stream turned out to be a series of shallow glides, falls and basins on hard metamorphic bedrock. *Calluna*, bell heather, ivy, bilberry and willow grew on the steep sides of the stream, and when I stopped to take a photograph, a fly hopped onto my thumb as if to introduce itself as one of the wildlife highlights of this refuge. 'This is where we live now,' it said, 'there is nowhere else on this side of the river.'

The finest pool of all was a two-foot-deep glitter under a narrow cascade of white water pouring from an undulating chute in the rock. I imagined children from the booley coming here in summer to splash about in this bracing water.

Birreencorragh

On my way up Glenlara, the summit of Birreencorragh (An Birín Corrach, the uneven point) was a distant, lofty shape glimpsed now and again through reels of passing cloud. It dominates the ridges rising around it from the west and south, while at the same time hanging back, withholding its presence and authority at some remove. Its magnificence, scale and elevation cannot be appreciated from the Glenlara side: instead, Birreencorragh should be seen as the culmination of a long, gradual ridge ascending to its summit from the north.

I had climbed it once before, coming up the ridge on the eastern side of Glenlara, and had stopped on the summit in the company of two other walkers on a warm April afternoon. I then headed off along the western ridge towards Mount Eagle, my destination that day, but I had glimpsed the imposing, stony flank of the northern approach. It struck me then like the rump, back and shoulders of some giant, mythical bull whose brow composed the summit at 698 metres. This analogy was reinforced in my mind by a comparable ridge coming off Croaghaun on Achill called Tóin a'Chruacháin, the rump of Croaghaun.

On any day of reasonable clarity, you can see this ridge from the Srahmore-Letterkeen side rising gradually across the eastern horizon: to climb it you have to drive around the mountain towards Keenagh. I started at the end of Glendavollagh (Gleann dá Mhullach, valley of the two summits), a deep, narrow valley like a trench cutting into the flank of the mountain from the east. The Deel River begins its life here as a mountain stream running east towards Crossmolina. From the map I measured four kilometres of ascent, from the start of the ridge above Keenagh to the summit, a steady, pure hypotenuse of unimpeded progress and fulfilment. The overgrazed, degraded hillside from my earlier walks at Glenlara had not prepared me for what I would encounter.

I scrambled down the gorge and crossed the river just above the forestry plantation: getting up the far side was a struggle because of deep heather, but I was grateful for this sign of health. The heather was deepest on the slope; when I got to the flat top, the going was easier. Three common heather species were there: the flowers of ling were reduced to little clenched purses; some of the bleached-out petals of bell heather had the delicacy of starched bonnets; cross-leaved heath had shut down its flowers for another year. A little higher up, at over 200 metres, crowberry, fir club moss and juniper appeared, giving a proper upland flavour to the vegetation. A bright lamp of sun blazed at me throughout, barely above the horizon, sometimes forcing me into a shady flank of the hill for respite.

This was the first hour, a patient, steady labour of embroidery, working my way across the rich fabric of ground, with no sight of my destination lost in the blinding dazzle of low December sun. My laughable fantasy of a geometric stroll along an easy incline had been replaced by an arduous, bedazzled slog through heather. The mass of Bullaunmore (An Ballán Mór, the big round hill, 388 metres) to my right, on the other side of Glendavollagh, was my marker, taking me past the 400-metre mark.

By now, height and exposure had reduced the profusion of heather. The ground was stonier, more exposed, the growth reduced to mosses, grasses and sedges subsisting in the lee of surface stones. The low, intense sun found galaxies of mica glinting in the grey rock. The calls of a single golden plover I disturbed from the slope were the essence of loneliness – and even these were diminishing, underlining my solitude.

The first prominent bulge on this ridge, corresponding to the rump of the great bull, is marked on the map as Nirkode, which sounds to me like a Bavarian bishopric (pronounced as three syllables) or an ancient surgical instrument (pronounced as two). As I approached a sheep fence that runs across the back of the ridge here, a chunk of dry stone wall caught my attention, and when I stepped over the sheep wire to get a closer look, there was another, greater astonishment: someone (how many?) had built two sections of wall, about five feet by five, with a neat door-sized gap between them forming an entrance. The purpose of this entrance, on an open slope at over 500 metres, was a complete mystery, something the place would not answer – it seemed that only fantasy could. Some of the rocks in this structure at waist height are massive, and could only have been lifted into place by several people, if we discount the megalithic heroes of Fenian times. Was this some ritual exercise of ancient power? Or an aristocratic folly subsidised by a Famine relief scheme?

A mouldering sheep fence turns towards the summit and runs for several hundred metres parallel to the spine of the ascending ridge; it would be a handy guide for anyone caught out in fog. As I walked on, the feeling of exposure and distance became extreme. I had few plants left to distract me, and no time to admire clumps of thrift colonising the bare ground; instead I was faced with the simple and almost overwhelming challenge of my progress along the back of the leviathan. I continued with a mesmerised sense that this was a ritual space ruled by an atavistic power where the walker was on trial, especially in the context of a short winter's day. From the rump to the shoulder of this beast was about a mile's walking on partly loose ground. Some patches of loose rock touched and tilted like clinkers.

The high point ahead appeared to be the summit, with a cairn on top, but something about it was not quite right, and I reached the shoulder with a gasp – the top was still some way off. The cairn at this shoulder (646 metres) was in fact the first in a series of waymarker cairns leading to the summit. With some time on my side, I kept going into a zone that dissolved identity and overwhelmed me. On the last section of slope before the top, the breeze fell, there was a ground cover of grassy sward, and it was almost warm. Then a few more steps and I was there on the summit, beside a nest of stones and a shattered trig point which I recognised from four years earlier.

The view from here is a 360° panorama of Mayo, from the Sheeffry Hills in the south, to the cliffs of the north coast, with Clew Bay, Achill and Corslieve in between. The plain to the east was as perfectly flat as Lough Conn itself, shimmering in the haze. The only high rival I could recognise was the bulky pyramid of Nephin (800 metres) off to the east, a solitary ship anchored away from the main fleet of peaks in the Nephin Beg Range. The silence was so complete as to be virtually abstract, scarcely challenged by an extreme penury of sound. A single call from a finch crossing the ridge – a snow bunting? A siskin?

The nest of stones forming the cairn is intriguing: it is as if the cairn had been partly levelled off and a hollow formed in the middle: I clambered over the rim and hunkered down in a four-metre-wide roofless hut. I decided this was a perfect place to have my sandwich, if not to undergo some rite of initiation. The mundane exercise of lunch was a way of controlling giddy feelings; otherwise I might have retreated, overcome by an immensity of scale. With the deep trench of Glendavollagh now just a varicose twist of a stream over a thousand feet below me, and the dark-shadowed corries of Corslieve in sequence to the north-west, I felt sure that the northern approach was the only way to climb Birreencorragh, along the spine of the great bull with its resonance from Iron Age cattle raids, and the rule of Queen Maeve, Connacht's legendary queen. As I sat on the brow of the beast, I believed that the cattle worshippers of ancient times could not have missed the symbolic power in the shape of this mountain.

This was my best pitch at prehistory, more immediate than any speculation about the origin and purpose of the stone structure, including the one I sat on. There was a measure of veneration, and also of sober caution, in the steps I took as I left the summit and returned along the stony ridge. Each stride called for quick judgement so as not to trip or sprain an ankle: this head-down concentration kept me distracted from wider views as I came down. Eventually, having passed the mysterious ruined gateway, I dropped down into Glendavollagh by a quicker route, a kind of staircase descent through heather deep enough for nesting grouse. I did not see any of these birds, only a few scattered droppings, enough to tell me they were there in small numbers.

The increasing whisper of the stream was a kind of welcome life, which I staggered across to reach the road. Along this section the juvenile river cuts a deep gorge into the bedrock through a succession of pools and white-water pourings. The overhanging slope, known in Irish as an allt, has a covering of deep heather and a scattering of trees, including some rowans sleeved in chocolate-coloured lichens, the emergent tips of the branches elegantly silver. As if to confirm the rich network of life in this place, a woodcock took off from rushes at the riverbank and showed rich tawny tail feathers on its way to cover farther up the slope; then a small falcon – probably a merlin – flickered briefly at the top of the ridge and disappeared across the heathery bluff. There was one more token of wonder: a beehive in a fenced enclosure near the road; it suggested heather honey, a sweetness that winter had stored away like a secret or a lover's promise.

Three days later I was back in Glendavollagh, looking for a pair of glasses in their case, which I thought I had lost from my rucksack in a bad-tempered tussle with a fence near the river. After a brief scramble down and a careful wading across I found the black case nested in grass, slightly damp but undamaged.

The river was higher than before, following more rain during the week. As I set out up the glen, a large sparrowhawk was patrolling low across the heather-clad hillside, harrier-like, after grouse. A distant skein of golden plover turned tinily above the ridge at about 400 metres, looking for a place to settle. The valley widened to a flat bottom of pasture, with stone levees taking the river in chuckling turns past grazing sheep. Two or three outpost farmhouses kept vigil in their deep seclusion under Birreencorragh; here I made a few enquiries of the first man I met. A pack of small, lean, vulpine border collies fussed around us as we stood in his yard. The ancient doorway stood out on the ridge above us like a tiny snag on the horizon. 'The tower,' he called it; he had lived all his life in the valley and had no idea who built it or what it was for. As for the cup-shaped cairn on the summit, he thought that hill walkers had had fun one day making a shelter from the cairn of loose stones.

I came away after that, strolling back down the valley to the deep section of the gorge. The river flows over bedrock here; centuries of floods have worn deep channels into the quartzite; layering in the rock has resulted in slabs and steps for water to bend round and pour over in a series of short cascades and streams. I came to the deepest, most dramatic section of the gorge and sat down.

The river hurries down through a narrowing gully in a sequence of seven small falls, each pouring a tawny froth onto the next ledge. The twenty-foot high outcrop of quartzite opposite was topped with a deep mop of ling and a decaying rowan. The lower ledges were a rich garden of plants growing here in spray and permanent shade: ivy, bilberry, woodrush, holly, spleenwort and ferns. Some ivy leaves had changed from pale greens and yellows into marbled russets and browns with a wet lustre.

As my pen enquires about these wonders, a fly arrives on the page and gropes about slowly, as if bewildered by the late season, and by its own survival. Perhaps it registered me as another animal and was drawn to my smell?

I stay in the constant rumble of the Falls of Deel, my name for this picturesque moment. Water from the wide pool at my feet spreads to the shallow rim flowing glassily, rapidly over scuffed boulders the colour of wolf pelt. A brief shudder of antique memory reminds me that at one time it would not have been safe to sit out here unarmed and alone. Then the waters rush into two narrow braids of foaming stream and run headlong round a corner into the lower gorge. A trout's tail flickers briefly on the surface, like a gesture at old times when pools like these would have been full of spawning fish.

At first I noticed a cloying smell of rotting flesh leaking into the calm air, but then a breeze fluttered through in mid-afternoon, scouring the gorge of its smells, and my chilling hands reminded me of my need for shelter and warmth. The picturesque finds its limits. I blow the fly off the page and leave. Just as I stepped back onto the road, I found the source of the smell: a stripped sheep carcass, with just a shrunken head and a neat foot sticking out from a mass of black and white fleece.

The grey ribbon of road dipped and rose across darkening moorland between Keenagh and the lake at Bunaveelagh. The last light of day was struggling in the distance behind monstrous clouds. A man walked back to his house where a fire was already lit, with peat smoke from the chimney swirling away. Another night of wind and rain was forecast. The place was being deserted; I was on my way home, and the few people left were turning to their stoves, TVs and computer screens. A winter's night was claiming the place, draining it of colour and warmth for all but the most exceptional explorer. I felt that there were more revelations stored within this brew of swirling, wet air. At Letterkeen I passed a hillside crested with tall stands of larch and spruce from the early days of forestry here, trees that might never be harvested, shadowy forms where a long-eared owl might hoot in a few weeks, claiming a territory. An entire wilderness can be conjured by such things, like a polar bear seen by Horatio Clare on Svalbard, 'the creation and the meaning of her landscape, a miraculous iteration of the place.'[33] But unlike Clare's polar bear, 'a pearl framed in the wilderness', the owl that could transform the setting might never be seen, but be given only to a patient listener.

I wanted to return to Birreencorragh and get another sense of the mountain from a different approach, this time from the south-east. I had seen Knockaffertagh (Eafartach's mountain?) from the top of Birreen, an imposing hill with a rocky escarpment like a collar round its head; I felt it like a surveyor's duty to walk the ground and look at the main mountain from that perspective. The forecast for the coming days was not good; the chances of meeting anyone on that hillside in mid-December were remote – it was going to be a lonely venture. The walk might have an interest of its own, but it would also be governed by Nan Shepherd's maxim that some lesser hills are worth climbing for the view they provide of the major summits.

I drove east from Newport through grey, blustery air. Lough Beltra was brimming from recent rain, and the Crumpaun River was in high spate: there was a sense of all colour being leached out of the world under winter's spreading influence of dark and cold; the flowing air mass was coming from the north. The weatherman mentioned wintry showers.

I crossed a new tourist stile on the Keenagh loop and got onto an old hill track leading into a dip between Knockaffertagh and another hill to the south. The air was full of the susurration of streams coming off the hill, the biggest hidden under wine-splashes of birch in a deep gully. The ridge above me had steep, heather-clad sides crossed by a first raven. I left the stone track and started into the climb, picking my way through collapsed masts of bracken and deep *Calluna*. Grouse, I was thinking, as a rainbow announced the arrival of a shower, a thin, ephemeral affair which drifted in, with blue sky behind it to the north.

After the first breast of the ridge, the ground eased away to a series of wide hollows with excellent cover and – as if on cue – a grouse took off silently, then a snipe, while a raven distracted me farther off on the horizon: in an instant the hillside had come alive, an excellent piece of upland terrain, with candelabras of fir club moss, and rich mats of crowberry spreading through the heather.

I stopped at about 350 metres in the shelter of a knotted face of quartzite to have a drink and take a look at Glendorragha (An Gleann Dorcha, the dark valley), the wide bowl encompassed by Birreencorragh's southern embrace. Rain moved through Glendorragha, not the irritating patter of drops on my rain jacket, but a slow-motion drift of water through space. The light found other ways through these veils and banks of grey cotton: sun above Lough Beltra sent searchlight shafts over land and water; it blazed on the glitter with an intense magnesium glow and suspended the wooded islands of the lake in a distant, picturesque antiquity.

I carried on across more hollows and inclines in a contest with tiredness. It took a dose of Walter Mitty fantasy to push me on from here: my breathlessness was because of thin air, the heather was Himalayan snow, my pauses for rest were necessary at altitude… the fantasy did its job and got me to the first patch of scree. The ground became stonier, with the dry friction underfoot of stones worn from exposure; and there, on the exposed knuckle of a ridge at 400 metres, a heap of grouse droppings where a bird had been roosting a few weeks earlier. Why here, in such raw terrain, and not in the cosier hollows farther down?

There is a series of waymarker cairns, like those on Birreencorragh itself, taking you through the last hundred metres of altitude to the top at 510 metres. These heaps of quartzite might be just a jolly boy-scout gesture from the twentieth century, clearly designed to get you to the top in mist, but there are also some low, ancient boundary walls nearby, suggesting rituals or territories from ancient times. And here, as another marker of antiquity, several deep bands of quartz run through the quartzite, on an east-west axis, like stripes across the hill; weather and ritual impulses have dismantled and disturbed much of this, but large amounts remain.

Although the wind had risen to a gale on the exposed hilltop, the wintry, overcast conditions made the quartz brighter, even in its greying form, like residues of snowmen during a thaw.

I staggered about, to get a few pictures. The lower skirts of scree extended below the cloud, with falls of white water in the folds of the pleats. White water. White quartz. A lumpy cobbling of grey rock, with moss deposits of curry-gold powder topped with heather brown.

With my energies revived, and the wind now at my back, I retraced my steps among the waymarker cairns and started the descent. Then a flock of golden plover appeared, eight of them working their way up the slope and passing me, as if they were supplying an answer to my colour queries: gold, they said, our gold is the best camouflage; you would never find us when we are settled on this ground. The plovers in their winter plumage had pale underparts, making them look leaner, as if their black summer bellies were a weight they had abandoned for the asperities of winter. I think they are superb, the embodiment of this place, its essence at any time. They must feed on lower wetlands at this time of year and fly up to the security of the hilltops to roost – what else could bring them up here? 'If there is one bird call,' wrote Nan Shepherd, 'that for me embodies the spirit of the mountain, it is the cry of the golden plover running in the bare and lonely places.'

There is a small rock quarry beside the track at the bottom of the slope, and a simple stone shed made from this local material a hundred metres away. There, on a low wall near the doorway, a wren called and popped into view. He scolded a few times, flew down to the doorway and pottered about in a mess of shitty straw where a few flies kept him fed in winter. The shed itself must be his winter roost. I was glad to have my winter day crowned by the King of the Birds at his castle under Knockaffertagh.

I came back through water sounds, where a full stream poured like a running engine into a culvert and hid its gleam in a thicket of golden fuchsia.

After that day on Knockaffertagh I wondered about other places in that part of Mayo, between Corslieve in the west and Lough Conn in the east, that partly industrialised, partly forested, partly abandoned, partly wild stretch of plain – with a few lakes and one or two hills, including Tristia (322 metres). (This obscure name has been explained as deriving from an equally obscure Irish word troiste, but it rings truest for me as a figuration of the sadness felt by some classically attuned settler looking out at the grey mists dissolving this lonely hill.) I had found unexpected wonders on a hill I visited out of a sense of duty, to investigate a higher complex of slopes, peaks and ridges. However, looking north and east, there were other unexplored surfaces: fragments of old blanket bog, flow country with locháns where I could set my compass and be away for hours, leaving roads behind. And with no way of knowing what I might encounter, only that the day would offer something out of the wastes of bog myrtle and molinia. The lonely cry of a bird. A fern in the grass. The remains of a live kill, or of a carcass. Cloud shapes.

To whittle everything down, to remove any pleasing scenic prospect, to avoid places where wildlife might be expected to congregate, to exclude any chance of a meeting with someone who might tell a story – to pare everything down to a movement over flat, limitless terrain, and see how far such an abstraction might take me before being confounded.

Nephin

'The mountain's gone wild,' said the farmer I met when I got back to the car. He was a sheepman who had seen changes to the vegetation on his commonage on the southern side of Nephin since the end of headage payments. The expansion of sheep headage payments during the 1980s and 90s saw a huge increase in sheep numbers over the western uplands, with the result that large areas were completely denuded of vegetation. In some places, the blanket bog had been reduced to bare peat with a meagre growth of sphagnum and mat grass (*Nardus stricta*), the least nutritious of upland grasses. Newsworthy photo-opps from the time showed politicians in wellingtons being shown badly affected sites by wildlife service officers.

The greedy, heedless abuses of sheep headage schemes may be a thing of the past, with vegetation – especially heather – recovering widely, but you can still marvel at the destruction of our uplands in many parts of Wild Nephin, where the term 'sheepwrecked' still applies.

The sheepman and I were custodians of two different ideas of wilderness: for him, a mountain going wild meant a loss of control, the landscape unrestrained by husbandry; for me, a mountain gone wild was something that quickened my imagination: it suggested that natural life was repairing with the return of plant and animal communities. The two meanings of wilderness, as primal chaos or as healing profusion, are at least as old as the sixteenth century, where they are dramatised in Shakespeare's plays. (*King Lear* and *A Midsummer Night's Dream* are examples of these polarities.) Either way, the healthy state of our recovering uplands is an outcome of human intervention, of changes in policy and practice. *The wild can be human work.*

Not that it is ever possible to view something as truly wild, because things in the natural world have been so elaborately conditioned by our own evaluations, imaginings and representations. Nephin itself first appeared on my horizon years ago in the middle of winter as a snow-capped pyramid, far away to the north, which I had time to marvel at only briefly on my daily commute to Castlebar. It always triggered an Irish proverb in my mind: 'Nuair a bhíonn sneachta ar Néifinn bíonn sé fuar in Éirinn; when there's snow on Nephin it's cold in Ireland.' The proverb is associated with Achill, where snow melts more readily under the influence of the milder sea, leaving Nephin's white cap in lonely eminence on the eastern horizon.

I first climbed it almost twenty years ago on a summer's day – a headlong, exuberant rush to the summit with relatives, following the western route. That brief, heedless moment of conquest then faded in the memory until the name Nephin and the need to cover my projected territory brought me back to it.

The derivation from Gaulish Nemetona, the goddess of the sacred grove, brings with it the allure of pre-Christian antiquity and suggests an ancient topography of beliefs and rituals, but the lack of evidence here is tantalising. Apart from the Dumnonii of Iorrus Domnann, who imported Nemetona to north Mayo, the early records for pre-Christian Connacht are, in the words of Dáibhí Ó Cróinín, 'almost non-existent'. We are confined to a few Patrician references and to inferences from tradition and folklore. St Patrick's early memorist Tíreachán, who hailed from Tirawley, makes a unique topographical reference in his mention of a woodland, Silva Vocluti, in that barony, where the saint is said to have met a son of Amolgid. Nollaig Ó Muiraíle thinks that this wood of Fochloth might have been at Foghill, near Kilalla; in reality the only meagre insight we can distill from Tíreachán's reference to his being a member of 'the great church of St Patrick in Silva Vocluti' is that there was a sanctity attaching to this woodland in the early Christian period and that this is consistent with a pre-Christian veneration in the figure of Nemetona.

Mayo's traditions concerning St Patrick are concentrated on Croagh Patrick, with its drama of the expulsion of snakes and noxious creatures from the island, and the overthrow of Lughnasa's Crom Dubh. Nephin, by contrast, has no such associations, and there is apparently no Lughnasa tradition on its summit. The observance of Lughnasa is attested, however, on the nearby hill of Tristia to the north-east, at 322 metres a much more community-friendly destination for a popular festival than the forbidding summit of Nephin.

While the Christian rebranding of Lughnasa took place most famously on Croagh Patrick, a much quieter succession is marked at St Patrick's Well in the valley at the foot of Tristia, looking across to the main bulk of Nephin itself. Here, there are two dark eyes of water in close proximity, one dedicated to St Patrick, the other to St Bridget. A modern notice gives details of prayers and movements to be observed in the performance of a station here, under the commanding horizon of the mountain. There's something compelling in the imperative of the high mountain at this site, which I felt recently, as I skipped and tiptoed across the soggy ground after a day's rain.

If Nephin has claims to being a holy mountain in a pre-Christian tradition, that does not imply that its rituals ever involved climbing to the top. There are several examples of sacred summits around the world where climbing is taboo.

It was in this spirit, in deference to native Australian culture, that Uluru (Ayers Rock) was closed to tourist climbers in October 2019. The Buddhist cult of Crystal Mountain, Dakpa Sheri, in south-east Tibet involves a lot of ritual activity within sight of the snow-capped summit, which has never been climbed.

One strand of the etymology of Nephin refers to a sacred wood or grove rather than to a mountain. In the Celtic, pre-Christian era of the Dumnonii, the lowland areas must have been extensively wooded, with the exception of the richer limestone country to the north, where settlement and clearance took place from Neolithic times, judging from the concentration of megalithic monuments. In contrast, the poorer land to the west and south was never as densely settled, and must have retained its wild character. Glen Nephin to the south runs south-west/north-east between Beltra Lough and Lough Conn. Its valley floor is remarkably flat, with no drumlins and few esker ridges of any elevation to offer ancient peoples secure routes through. As the valley shares its name with the mountain, Glen Nephin must surely have been the wooded landscape to which the name refers.

Nowadays, with much of the valley reclaimed for intensive sheep farming, it takes a special effort of imagination to see a wild, impenetrable *Urwald* stretching away from the mountain as far as the 395-metre hill of Farbreiga (fear bréige, literally fake man, scarecrow) and the large sheets of fresh water to the east, Loughs Conn and Cullin. As regards the rituals that might have been observed here by devotees of Nemetona, the wildwood has kept them a secret as far as I know.

Part of Nephin's impact is its isolation as the highest standalone mountain in Ireland, at some remove from the peaks and ridges of the Nephin Beg Range. When compared with other peaks such as Corslieve, Birreencorragh and Ben Gorm, Nephin is easy to drive round to get views from every angle, and there are three main trails up the mountain where you begin climbing almost as soon as you leave the car, without a long fag to the mountain's base.

My perspective on the mountain is shaped by its appearance as I view it from my home to the south-west (I no longer commute to Castlebar). In this aspect it appears in shape like a limpet, a not-quite-symmetrical cone, something that might have inspired Paul Henry, a mountain abstraction of distance, with varieties of shade and illumination depending on the clarity of the atmosphere. Atmospheric conditions can produce variations in visibility, so that the mountain appears strikingly closer at certain times. This has been plausibly explained to me as the effect of sudden clarity, on a day when the air is free of moisture and the eye can appreciate details that are usually obscured by humidity: 'Our brain uses clarity as a cue for judging distance so when we look at something through a few miles of air, the level of clarity impacts on how we judge distance, so very clear things look closer.'[34] This view is corroborated by the artist Benita Stoney, who wrote to me, about the influence of air mass on colour outdoors, that when the wind is in the humid south-west, 'you can't see anything at all.' She notices colours at their richest and deepest when the wind is in the dryer north or north-west.

When I asked a number of people I met in the vicinity of Nephin about this, I was consistently told that when the mountain looks close, it was a sign of rain on the way; on the other hand, 'in fine weather she sits back and relaxes.' I found this belief repeated in the archive of the 1930s Schools Folklore Scheme for the area; I have also heard of it from people living in sight of Croagh Patrick, from the Ox Mountains in Sligo, and the Blackstairs Mountains in south Leinster. I am inclined to put this down to a native tendency towards negativity, where people fatalistically predict a change for the worse; but there may be another atmospheric reason, which is widely reported by travellers in the Arctic. In areas where land masses and water bodies are usually cold, objects can appear higher, or closer, than they actually are because of light refraction. Light rays are refracted when warmer air passes over a cold surface or layer, as it does during temperature inversion: this causes objects to be lifted above their actual position. In the extremes of arctic conditions, these so-called superior mirages can cause objects below the horizon to be lifted up and become visible, as happened in a number of famous cases with images of ships. The same phenomena can play havoc with perceptions of distance and scale. Kathleen Jamie reports watching a shape on the Alaskan tundra which she took to be either a bear or a woman until it took off – a raven. In our climate, a change in weather sending warm air across a cold surface of land or water could produce this effect of refraction, bringing the mountains closer.

The limpet shape of Nephin seems to correspond to its appearance on the modern OS map, with densely packed ten-metre contours rising steeply from the surrounding roads. In reality, the mountain is a much flatter massif: if it were really shaped like a limpet, a mountain almost five kilometres broad at its base would be about 3,000 metres high, or three times the height of Carrauntoohil.

Its longest, north-western face is an imposing whaleback interrupted at the end by a huge corrie, Fionn's Chair, falling directly from the summit. This corrie, formed originally by snow accumulation in the sheltered lee of the summit, is conspicuous on clear days in winter as a depression in deep shadow. No sunlight reaches the bowl of this depression for weeks in winter. This cold northern edge of Nephin, which is also marked by forestry plantation at lower levels, is known locally as Canada. The eastern face is much shorter than the long northern ridge, and presents a series of low escarpments overlooking the village of Lahardaun.

While the ridges of Nephin above Lahardaun are marked by glacial action during Ireland's last Ice Age, the village remembers a much more recent, traumatic event, also involving glacial ice. On the night of 14th April 1912, the *Titanic* collided with a large iceberg off the coast of Newfoundland and sank over two hours later. Among the 2,224 passengers and crew on board were fourteen people from townlands around the mountain, in the parish of Addergoole. Eleven of them perished in the tragedy, while three of the women were rescued and survived. For some years, there has been an active local committee involved in commemoration and remembrance of the disaster, and in 2012 an imposing Titanic Memorial Park was opened in the village, in the shadow of Nephin. The park features four life-sized bronze figures representing departing emigrants bound for the US, and a shiny bronze model of the ship's prow, approximately sixteen feet high.

The iceberg that sank the *Titanic* on its maiden voyage had originated in Greenland, where it had 'calved off' one of the glaciers of the ice sheet on reaching the sea. It had then been borne by Arctic sea currents running south from there across the Labrador Sea towards Newfoundland. In April 1912, the spread of sea ice and icebergs in the Atlantic off Newfoundland was particularly extensive owing to variation in sea currents in an area where the Gulf Stream interacts with colder Arctic currents from the north. Transatlantic shipping in the north-western Atlantic would exchange telegraph messages with information about sea ice, but the protocols for these transmissions were lax, as later enquiries discovered. One important message about icebergs was received by an overworked wireless operator shortly before the collision, but was not acted upon immediately. The look-outs in the ship's crow's nest were reliant on the naked eye as they peered into the moonless night and saw the iceberg only when it was too close to avoid – the sea was calm at the time, and without a white jabble of wave action at the base of the icebergs they were particularly difficult to make out. In the event, the effort to avoid the huge iceberg came too late, and the ship was fatally damaged.

On the eve of their departure for Cobh (Queenstown), people gathered in the emigrants' houses to celebrate what was known at the time as the 'American Wake'; the term suggests that the people leaving for North America would never be seen again. In actual fact, by 1912, the emigrant path to American cities such as New York and Chicago was not all one-way traffic.

Catherine Bourke of Carrowskeheen, who drowned when the liner sank, had previously worked in Chicago from 1905 to 1910. At the time of the disaster she was pregnant with her first child. She had boarded one of the lifeboats, but got back onto the stricken ship to be with her husband John, whom she had recently married 'for better or for worse', and who was being refused permission to join her on the lifeboat. (The same impulse of loyalty impelled Catherine's sister-in-law Mary to give up the chance of survival: she left the same lifeboat to stay with her brother.) Another victim, Catherine McGowan, had also worked in Chicago, where she ran a successful boarding house, and had returned home to chaperone her young niece Annie McGowan, on her trip to America. Annie, who was among the three out of fourteen who survived, was herself a US citizen by birth; her family had brought her back to the parish when she was two years of age. A fourth woman, Mary Mangan of Carrowskeheen, had also worked for a time in the US, had recently become engaged there, and had come back to Ireland to visit her elderly mother. Her body was recovered and identified, only to be given a 'sea burial'.

These and other details from this harrowing and poignant story give the impression of an enterprising, outward-looking community who were well informed about the life that awaited them in the New World. Delia McDermott, from Knockfarnaght to the east of the mountain, had bought a new outfit and hat, which her mother insisted she wear on arrival in New York in order to look smart. Having boarded a lifeboat at the start of the evacuation, Delia remembered her hat, and returned to her cabin to retrieve it; she then managed to board another lifeboat in the midst of all the pandemonium, and survived. Young James Flynn of Cuilkillew was not so lucky: following the 'women and children first' rule, he was barred from boarding a lifeboat where there was available space, and he also drowned, along with approximately 1,500 others, in the freezing waters.[35]

In my tentative enquiry of the mountain, I am drawn away from these deeply held memories in Lahardaun towards Nephin's southern side. As I approach from Lough Beltra and turn left at the townland of Boggy (Bogaigh, bogs), the pointed apex of the limpet subsides and Nephin presents a long flank running towards the townland of Cloughbrack

(Cloch Breac, speckled stone). These slopes facing the sun contain two smaller steep valleys or hollows in the embrace of imposing ridges and their broad skirts of scree: Lugnagroy (Log na Graí, hollow of the horses) and Lugnamannaun (Log na Mannán, hollow of the kid goats). The stream in Lugnagroy drains west into the Crumpaun River and Lough Beltra; the Lugnamannaun stream turns east, eventually joining Lough Conn and the Moy catchment. When viewed from below, these two narrow glens are partly hidden by the base of a spur separating them; as this spur rises to a shoulder at about 400 metres, it looks like a separate summit, known locally as the Small Hill. The back of this hill continues as a narrow ridge rising upwards towards the higher flank of the mountain, comprising the most dramatic part of this southern ascent.

I got there first in late September on an uplifting, high-chambered sort of day following a spell of miserable, wet weather in August and early September. Autumn was set in the brightness of red berries – rowan, holly, hawthorn – and the fading purples of scabious; when I sat down by the roadside to write a few notes, I heard grasshoppers churring on a stony bank and bursts of late song from a skylark and a passing chiffchaff. The mountaintop was clear; air was pouring across the world, as if Glen Nephin were the bed of a river and the air itself the current of a great, fast-flowing stream.

I felt that the mountain shaped a high geography of air through different levels around its bulk of stone and heather. The rising winds lift ravens, kestrels, and hooded crows, occasionally a buzzard, rarely an eagle. The mountain must also be a landmark for migrating birds such as swallows and house martins, and a few ospreys on passage between breeding grounds in Scotland and their winter quarters in West Africa.

My enquiries about eagles on Nephin have not yielded many results: a very few wanderers have been spotted there in recent years since the beginning of Ireland's reintroduction programmes, but I have not come across any historical references to eagles on Nephin. Nor are there any references to eagles in popular songs from the area. You have to look west, towards the massif of Birreencorragh, to find references to eagles in history and folklore. Around Nephin itself, the records are silent.

But I did elicit one precious insight from a sheepman I spoke to near Lahardaun: he had just returned from the National Ploughing Championships in Carlow where he met a Kerry sheep farmer who had sea eagles in his area: they talked about these birds, whose reintroduction had caused a lot of controversy at the outset, and the Kerryman assured him that the eagles were doing no harm. It was gratifying to know that these countrymen were making their own judgements on this vexed issue without interference from prejudice and stoked-up fears.

A month later, the skylark and chiffchaff were absent, and the bog vegetation was vivid following the first searings of frost. Ling and cross-leaved heath were over; just a few residual flowers were showing on bell heather. Here and there a yellow tormentil. A milkwort's sapphire star. The mountainside was putting on its winter colours.

My rambles in search of these colours and textures brought me back in late October and mid-November to the Small Hill between the two hollows, now a favourite, accessible stretch of ground.

The hill rises from the 100-metre contour line to about 400 metres, with a gentle eastern ascent above the new water scheme at Cloughbrack. The western side is shorter and steeper, giving the hill a 'humped' appearance, like the shoulders of a bull. In the clear light of winter, the lower stretches covered with bracken are a rich buff, with silver exclamations of bare rowan trees spread across the slope, like Birnam Wood advancing to Dunsinane. These stands of bracken have a tendency to snag the walker with their tough stems, but they are a refuge for the wren, and they cradle some rich basal foxglove leaves through the harsher times.

Just above the zone of bracken, as you enter the heath, there's a stage where purple moor grass (*Molinia*) is abundant in the heather; by October its leaves have withered and curled in blonde ringlets draping the heather stems, and they make a hissing sibilance on the hillside when the wind picks up – the second plant, after *Phragmites* reeds, I consciously understood as a sound. The heather cover here is healthy, with deep stands of older plants, their stems showing silver, like a miniature forest. Above the *Molinia* zone, the main assemblage is three species of heather (ling, bell and cross-leaved), with staghorn lichens, red sphagnum and deer sedge. Deer sedge is a favourite of mine: in winter it darkens to a rich teak, with paler patches on the stems, giving it a banded appearance; where it has not been grazed down, the stalks are as supple and pliant as a horse's mane. I found several sets of droppings from red grouse roosts on this ground, clumps of bleached-out cylinders in shallow depressions close to the Lugnagroy stream.

As exposure to the elements increases with altitude, and more stone shows on the surface, bearberry takes over as the signature plant intermixed with heathers and grasses.

Most of its berries are gone by mid-October, but when I found one intact I chewed it carefully, relishing its tang of imagined rock and water. Mat grass, the dominant plant of overgrazed bogs is here also, as isolated, bleached tufts, and in this context I celebrate its punk-peroxide style. Fir club moss, another plant of the heights, appears near the shoulder of the spur like a miniature conifer just a few inches high.

On my third visit in mid-November I was climbing this hill on its western flank, on the rim of a narrow gorge, when two finches flew across, headed for higher ground. I was thinking of snow bunting, a species of high mountains and exposed winter coasts. Half an hour later, a larger flock of about fifteen rose in the air above the river and rounded a rocky bluff. The clear chimes of their calls were unfamiliar, and it was not until I checked them on the internet that I was sure. In the desertion of the uplands in winter, the soundscape is sparse, but any small calls have the power to charm.

The presence of snow buntings on Nephin in winter opened up a whole new vista. I had seen them fleetingly on the north Mayo coast a few times, and celebrated them in my imagination years ago when they were still just a fascination gleaned from the first *Atlas of Breeding Birds in Britain and Ireland* (1976), where the entry said, 'In the vast expanses of mountain country it is difficult to keep track of the Snow Bunting population, but, ever since the first authenticated nest was discovered in 1886, this species has captured the imagination.' My own brief poetic annotation on the species was published in *The Clare Island Survey* (1991):

Snow Bunting

Before I could invoke
the snow buntings as snow-flakes

that settle from nowhere,
as fleckings on scree an echo away,

they had parleyed on me.
Relishing their *nivalis*,

I was climbing to conjecture
the merest Eden

when they deserted the stones, lichen, saxifrage
that were to host them.

The quotation from the *Breeding Atlas* refers to the Scottish Highlands, where a small breeding population has been studied for many years, but the fascination extends to Ireland, where snow buntings are winter visitors from Iceland and Scandinavia. They often reward a cold winter's walk along remote stretches of coast, and can even appear on snow-covered uplands. The Scottish writer Jim Crumley has described an encounter with snow buntings in heavy snow in winter at 3,000 feet in the Cairngorms: in the remote immensity of a famous corrie 'hung with unfathomable layers of snow', he came across a flock of about twenty feeding on tiny red spiders.[36]

In these islands, snow buntings are at the very southern end of their range and they share this biogeographical space with equally scarce species such as twite, red-necked phalarope and red-throated diver. As the most northerly breeding passerine in the world, they are a resilient species, the sparrow of Inuit settlements in the Arctic; their fleeting appearance in winter adds a special presence to windswept coasts and hilltops, and it was uplifting to discover them here, at an inland site in the west.

A spell of fine weather in late November finally gave me a chance to push on past the shoulder of the spur. I took the marked route starting at the Cloughbrack water scheme, following the ridge of the Small Hill. As I crossed the first stretch of stony ground after about an hour's walking, I heard a snow bunting's brief trill, like a little ritual bell, a summons to the holy mountain. By the time I got to the narrow ridge separating the two valleys, I was fully embraced by the higher mountainsides and their broad falls of scree. On this stony terrain, vegetation was flattened and stunted, with bearberry forced to crawl prostrate to avoid the elements. At 500 metres, I saw Glen Nephin as a bright floor of green-and-brown quilting; Beltra Lough was farther off, a platter of glare suspended in a velvet haze.

As time is precious on these short winter days, I was mindful of my turnaround deadline of one o'clock; I had an hour left as I made the last section of the ascent, counting the white sticks that some generous, thoughtful people had put there a couple of years earlier. Those fine lines at seventy-metre intervals served me as way- and mindmarkers: just keep moving, don't turn back now, four more and you'll be at the rim of the plateau.

Three ravens quartered the high rim of the glen, pronking and tumbling, to underline their ownership of these spaces. I checked each of them with my binoculars, hoping for an eagle to take shape among them. I've done this thousands of times in the Mayo mountains for thousands of ravens, hoodies and gulls – and three eagles. Two sea eagles on separate occasions at Letterkeen, and that unexpected, thrilling goldie in Glenlara last December. Three observations to add to a scant chronicle of their presence in Wild Nephin.

And then I am at the last marker, eye-level with the table-top. White zeppelins of cloud block the space for a few moments and then pass on. Distance is misted over, but I have a clear sight across stony rubble to a few low cairns of quartzite. The first of these is topped with a slab of bright quartz. And there to my right, nearer and more convenient than expected, is the concrete plinth of the trig point marking the top at 806 metres. There's still some drifted snow on the ground from a few days earlier, with the footprints of other walkers. This terrain is also densely marked by stone formations: circles and spirals as if in homage to Andy Goldsworthy, and faint traces of a few names subsiding into the overgrowth of moss. A partly collapsed curved section of wall shelters a makeshift stone bench in its arc – just enough for a brief rest, or an invitation to a brave camper to pitch a tent here on a night in summer.

I'm still busy with my camera phone, mindful of my schedule, as I approach the trig point and its tattered scrap of braid in the county colours. Then I step around it and my spirit nearly falls out through my eyes. I have blundered to the edge of 'a gulf... so profound that the mind stopped,' as Shepherd wrote of a similar moment in the Cairngorms. The great corrie of Fionn's Chair is there at my feet; if a gust of wind shouldered me off this ledge I could roll and slide for a thousand feet before the slope eased. My senses are in a rush to find their scale, like that moment in a film when a camera moves across a rooftop and then discovers the fall to street level hundreds of feet down.

I look again at my phone and hesitate before taking a photograph: the display shows the name of someone I shared a life with many years ago; in the same combination I glimpse a complete fetch of altitude and a reckoning of my years. I take a couple of quick snaps of the abyss and back away.

Something in the device knows about me; the screen prompt says, 'Try saying, "Take a selfie."' Whatever intelligence this is, – geolocation, or some algorithm that has processed my panoramic shots – I decline, as if I were beyond vanity here, if no vanity had compelled me to come here in the first place.

I mark the occasion instead by going back to the rough shelter, where I sit down and pour some hot tea from a flask. In the clear spaces among the snow just beyond my boots, a tight carpet of sedges and grass is coloured like golden tweed.

On the way back down, without the pressure of a schedule, I can take time to look at the ground I am on, and think about the expanses of bare scree on the steepest sides around me. The trail may not be as steep as the main areas of scree – which one farmer compared to the pitch of a slate roof – but there is a parallel process at work here, of stones moving down a mountain. The slope is littered with stones that have shifted from the peaty soil to reveal black sockets where each of them had lain for months or years. The severest gales and frosts of winter must play a part, but so too must the hooves of grazing animals and the boots of walkers gradually nudging these stones out of their resting places. My imagination adds all the animals and people that have moved across here since the last Ice Age: farmers, walkers, rebels, surveyors, hunters, sheep, goats, horses, foxes, hares, deer, dogs, and wolves; and I think of every stone pushed downward by their steps as their memorial, scattered all over these slopes.

I pass a few larger boulders, like mountains in miniature less than a metre high, which model this process on a smaller scale: small stones lie in smithereens on the ground around them, as if a sculptor had been working on the boulder top. Weather has played its part, with water in cracks and crevices freezing during the winter and bursting the seams open. I nudge one knob of rock with my toe and a fragment falls away, as I observe the slow disintegration of Nephin with a small gesture.

With such a conveniently marked route, there's little you could point to as danger here; just one stretch of the path crosses the top of an escarpment with a rubble of bare scree at its base. I stand there above a distant cypher of sheep, a flock of fourteen being herded across the top of the glen. A border collie slips across the slope towards them, as fluid in the heather as a fish. Then I spot the sheepman, who had announced the wilderness to me a few days earlier, following at his own steady, unhurried pace.

We're on a bright south-facing slope that was heated by the sun even during the Ice Age. The glaciers on this side were smaller than Fionn's Chair and sat higher on the mountain. They did not have the power to bulldoze the Small Hill out of the way, but their outwash carried material to the foot of the slope: gravels and boulders that are now exposed lower down at Cloughbrack. I admire these deposits topped with peat along the Lugnamannaun stream as I make my way back to the car.

NORTH

The Nephin Forest

I decided to shake off the froth of Christmas and walk to the Nephin Forest, taking the southern approach through Skerdagh and Glenlara. My plan was to climb up to Doo Lough on the saddle near Mount Eagle and descend into Glen Augh, but the day was drizzling and overcast, forcing me to keep to lower ground. Ní hé lá na fearthainne lá na sléibhe, a day of rain is not the day for the mountains, I said to myself, trialling a new proverb.

Since the downpours of November and early December, the weather had been mild, worryingly so. People on social media were reporting many plants in flower: we had snowdrops under the alders in the garden, and bluebells and narcissi shooting vigorously; Sibylle at Rock House had three-cornered leek in flower. This weather, more than reports of distant glaciers and ice-caps retreating, makes global warming a reality.

Jessica dropped me off at the forest in Glenlara and I set out along the track heading directly up the valley. There was a fullness, a vigour in the flowing streams that suggested rain in the night, though I hadn't heard it; I would stick to the forestry track for as long as possible to avoid the wet valley bottom.

The air was thick with mist and drizzle, with windows of clearance that closed again quickly: as the poet James Harpur put it, 'When the rain stopped, it started to rain.' After about a mile I stepped into the shelter of a stand of big spruce trees. Here I could sit and take in a rain-forest day. The air was veiled with a fine, silent mizzle drifting down slowly; it would not hide even the tiniest calls of goldcrest and wren. Where I was sitting, though, there was another noise from a full stream charging down through falls and little basins. Water in another form, as vapour, erased the higher slopes, dissolved sky and mountain ridge into subtle tones of grey. As the mizzle thickened, bright drops fattened at the end of twigs: they glistened and fell when ripe, making small soggy patterings in the grass. Then the drops tapped on my anorak, pecking at my securities, testing the precautions I had taken with raingear, footwear, plastic protection for my camera, phone, and sandwiches. I am not a creature of the rainforest, even though I detail all the manifestations of its element as cloud, mist, mizzle, drizzle, stream, flow, drop, drip and the dampness in my notebook that will have ruckled its pages by the end of the day.

The forestry track continues in a straight line to the top of the valley. Where the hard surface ends, a right turn took me down through a narrow gap in the conifers to the edge of the plantation. I crossed a sheep fence and a small stream to emerge onto open ground under Mount Eagle. I had left the Skerdagh Valley: the water was now flowing north into another catchment, towards Lough Feeagh and Burrishoole.

The rocky slope under Mount Eagle is much drier than the sphagnum-covered swamp in the hollow: I stepped along the scree, finding a path among the white lichen-splashed rocks, across a series of tiny streams off the hillside. Again, as so often, old walls and levees appeared in the lower ground, astonishing me with their obscure record of toil in this abandoned place. Then the south-eastern fringe of the Nephin Forest at Glen Augh appeared on the horizon as a dark line of mature lodgepole pine.

Nephin Forest is in fact a recent coinage, and has been adopted by people involved in the Wild Nephin Wilderness project. Wild Nephin was an idea first floated in 2012 by Coillte's then head of recreation, environment and public goods, Bill Murphy, to turn the Nephin Beg Range and its adjacent plantations into a designated wilderness. The wilderness idea was taken from North America in order to guarantee a vast area free of human intrusion; it had additional value as a reserve for nature conservation and biodiversity enhancement; the backers of the project also wanted to promote the Wild Nephin area as a destination for 'primitive recreation' where people could engage with the natural landscape.

The following year, a Memorandum of Understanding (MOU) was agreed between Coillte and the National Parks and Wildlife Service, to run for fifty years, and allow for the management of the National Park lands and the adjacent Nephin Forest as a wilderness area. The MOU started out with a programmatic definition of the wilderness idea:

> A wilderness is a large, remote, wild (or perceived wild), protected and publicly owned landscape with good visual and natural qualities. A wilderness facilitates humans to experience our connections to the larger community of life through the enjoyment of nature, solitude and challenging primitive recreation, without significant human presence or the intrusion of human structures, artefacts or inappropriate activities while supporting a functioning ecosystem.

A wilderness is therefore generally free from human management and manipulation, and is an area where, through rewilding, natural processes are gradually restored. A wilderness can include modified landscapes that no longer support long-term human occupation. A wilderness should be a minimum of 2000 ha, offering opportunities for solitude and primitive recreation.

The MOU is an ambitious and – in an Irish setting – possibly unique attempt at securing an extensive wild landscape for conservation and recreation. The time lines are generous: a lease of fifty years and a transition period of fifteen years from 2018 to 2033, recognising the pace of rewilding processes. It also represents a ground-breaking move by the huge landowner, Coillte, to share in the aims of nature conservation. Such a high-profile move by the state's forestry company has of course drawn all sorts of comment and criticism in the public arena; however, short of the negativity that generally distorts public debate, there are many elements in the project that give pause.

The legal formulations of the MOU have their cultural origins in an American ideal of wilderness as it was focussed and articulated by thinkers such as John Muir, the founder of the Sierra Club, and the inspirational driver of the movement to establish National Parks such as Yosemite and Yellowstone in the US. While this impulse towards immersion in an intact wilderness had unrivalled scope in the pristine landscapes of the American West, its origins were recognisably meta-Christian, and descended from radical Protestant currents of thought. As Simon Schama has shown in *Landscape and Memory* (1995), the early white explorers of the Mariposa Grove in the Sierra Nevada, where redwoods and pines predated the life of Christ, thought that they had entered a new Eden, which the New World had granted them to compensate for the corruptions of modern European history. In cultural terms, this wilderness idea largely erased the legacy of the Native American peoples who had lived, hunted and kept their traditions for many centuries in the same lands. (Even the romanticism that belatedly recognised the integrity of these indigenous cultures was unable to save them from virtual annihilation.)[37]

This North American model of wilderness was given statutory definition in the US Wilderness Act of 1964, and was imported into European policy via the EU's 2008 Wilderness in Europe Report and a subsequent resolution of the European Parliament. In this way, the American wilderness ideal became filtered by Brussels-speak into a legal discourse embedded within other European Union measures, such as the Habitats Directive, which set up the Special Areas of Conservation (SAC), and the Birds Directive. Independently of these European frameworks, Wild Nephin National Park was established as a Category II Park under an International Union for Conservation of Nature protocol where 'a protected area must exclude exploitation or occupation that is not consistent with the purpose of the designation,' which effectively means that all lands within the National Park are owned by the state and that this precludes management agreements between farmer-occupiers and the parks and wildlife service.

The Wild Nephin Wilderness is therefore a construct of policy rather than a discovery: the MOU declares that 'The ultimate goal of the conversion project is that *Wild Nephin will become a wilderness* (my emphasis).' It is clear that wilderness as a pitch into the future is completely different from wilderness as the discovery of a pristine landscape before human intrusion. As such, the Wild Nephin project is aligned with a different, more recent idea of rewilding: this involves allowing natural habitats to revert to a wild state, with possible management measures to reintroduce animals that have become extinct, or to remove signs of modern human intrusion. Rewilding is a process that has also taken place in many landscapes that have been abandoned or set aside for other reasons, such as the Brecklands of Cambridgeshire, where Helen Macdonald watched displaying goshawks at the start of her memoir, *H is for Hawk*, and declared that 'The wild can be human work.' By that she signalled that rewilding can be either a deliberate outcome of protection or a by-product of neglect.

The official documents that define the wilderness project are bristling with definitions, measures, and declarations about the competencies of various state agencies, but before broaching any more of this detail, it makes sense to resume our approach to the Nephin Forest itself, to draw aside the veil of official policy and see some of the reality.

After my walk along the open hillside under Mount Eagle, where my birding tally was a single snipe, the grove of lodgepole pine was a fine embroidery of bird calls and songs: goldcrest, coal tit, dunnock, robin, song thrush and wren. Compared with the desolation of the open hillside, the forest holds the promise of life and variety; to get a better view of that prospect, I have to go back a few weeks to late December and climb from the same point in Glen Augh towards Mount Eagle in Jessica's company.

Glen Augh (an obscure name, pronounced a-hoo, with the same intonation as 'cashew') has become one of my favourite corners of the Nephin Forest. It is reached by turning right after the bridge over the Srahrevagh River, following the sign for Jamesie's Well. The forest here dates back to 1951, as we were cheerfully informed by one of the locals whose father was involved in the very earliest phase of afforestation in north Mayo. As you walk or drive up the valley of the Srahrevagh River (An Sraith Riabhach, the grey or gloomy srah), the monotony of recent re-plantings is broken by older stands of lodgepole pine and spruce, and a varied topography along the river itself, where Coillte planted birch and oak about ten years ago as part of a trial to see if the biodiversity of the area could be enhanced. Some of the very oldest lodgepole pines are now impressive trees almost seventy years old and stand along the track as bearers of a promise of what rewilding can bring to this area: in management terms, the Nephin Forest in Glen Augh will benefit from 'long term retention' of existing trees.[38]

After we parked at the south-western end under Gogín, we pushed our way through a narrow strip of replanted spruce to get to open ground: a steep slope above the track brought us to the ridge leading to the top of Gogín. From here, we could see the main upper section of the glen, spread out in several zones of various ages, reaching most of the way to the so-called Top of Leana (léana, a meadow or field), a western limb of the Birreencorragh massif.

Rain had been forecast, but in the end it never arrived and we were treated to calm conditions – a high, nacreous sky still blushing with early light as we climbed. Scarves of lower mist were draped over the hillsides while other banks of cloud vapour moved into the glen, threatening to spill over us, but the ridge we were on stayed clear. Banks of mist drifting at lower levels give a new sense of space: a two-kilometre-wide valley you look across in transparent weather is transformed into a volume of its own, full of travelling shapes and draperies. The space becomes occupied by a theatre of forms, with varying portions of forest and hill appearing and disappearing. To the north-west and west, the higher summits of Ben Gorm, Nephin Beg and Corslieve appeared like dark rocks washed by a surf of cloud. To the east, the long ridge of Birreencorragh appeared only briefly behind a smoulder of mist.

The Nephin Forest was spread to the north for fifteen kilometres as far as the disused peat workings at Bellacorick. It covers much of what Robert Lloyd Praeger celebrated in the 1930s as the Bog of Erris:

> Where else in Ireland will you find 200 square miles which is houseless and roadless – nothing but brown heather stretching as far as you can see, and rising along a kind of central back-bone into high bare hills breaking down here and there in rocky scarps, with the Atlantic winds singing along their slopes?[39]

Praeger was writing before the Irish state spread its modernising influence into the area, with peat extraction for energy generation and large-scale afforestation. The heather-clad wilderness of Praeger's day, with its patchwork of locháns and lakes, has been completely transformed, with sheep overgrazing from EU grant schemes adding to the burdens on the landscape. As another sign of this landscape's alignment to the modern world, the white blades of wind turbines near Bellacorick flail continually on the northern horizon.

Almost eighty years after Praeger wrote, the American wildlife writer Jeremy Miller walked into this forest from the western side at Scardaun, and was dismayed at the sight of clear-felling in the Nephin wilderness: 'the scale of the logging was jarring and hard to reconcile with an attempt to return the land to a more natural state. To my eye, in fact, the scene looked no different to industrial clear cutting in the Cascade Mountains.'[40] Miller's perplexity is partly explained by the fact that Coillte will continue some logging operations during the transfer phase from 2018 to 2033, before NPWS takes over. In the meantime, the Wild

Nephin Forest continues to be a place of clashing recognitions, between the war zone of clear-felling and the kind of wildness Miller found in another spot: 'an idyllic stand of old-growth conifers and hardwoods along a meandering river.'[41]

The conifer plantations are dense and regular across much of this vast tract, but there are scatterings of isolated trees on the hillsides and some old stands that have been left to grow on. This scene, of mountain and conifer, is like an American image and appeals to that part of our imagination that has been shaped by the cinematic wild west of North America and the frontier of the Rocky Mountains. With its Alaskan sitka spruce and its north-west American lodgepole pine, the Nephin Forest is a piece of imported picturesque; because of its place in our TV- and film-savvy minds, it is a much more marketable wilderness than the unimpeded spaces of the wild river catchments, Tarsaghaunmore and Owenduff, to the west of the Nephin Beg Mountains.

All this makes the idea of restoration entirely problematic. If you were trying to restore the great flow peatlands of the Bog of Erris you would be faced with the impossible task of removing the entire forest. Even if your aim was woodland restoration you would have to eliminate sitka and lodgepole in favour of broadleaves, Scots pine, and yew, another impossible and scientifically questionable task. In reality, the Wild Nephin Wilderness is an unprecedented project in Irish terms: to manage a woodland legacy where the main tree species are non-native, North American conifers. Given that forestry normally removes trees after about forty years, the prospect of a conifer forest over seventy years old in the West of Ireland is something entirely new. But this does not make it uninteresting or invalid. On the contrary. A maturing, and one day ancient pine and spruce forest is an exciting prospect, and runs counter to the environmental argument that coniferous forestry is bad news. We already have crossbills, siskins, coal tits, red deer and pine martens, and as the rewilding process continues, more birds and animals are likely to arrive, even without deliberate reintroductions. Jays are a welcome arrival; great spotted woodpeckers are spreading in Ireland and will colonise the Nephin Forest one of these days. Then there are further colonists: ospreys, sea eagles and goshawks which I believe can be at home here given protection and with more enlightened public attitudes. In short, the Nephin Forest does not fit within the essentially conservative set of scientific habitat classifications, but will become a habitat class of its own, a mosaic of continuous and open forest, blanket bog, broadleaf woodland, and mountain.

It was with this future in our minds that we stood there, looking north across the forest towards Nephin Beg and Corslieve. That December day with Jessica was a great contrast to my solitary, face-freezing climb from Glenlara. From the top of Gogín we strolled towards Mount Eagle with the entire ridge to ourselves, as is usually the case in that area: our empire of solitude was checked only by a plastic pouch containing two small religious medals Jessica found on the mossy ground. I held it up for a few moments before returning it to its resting place, admiring its own quiet veneration of this spot, though the image of the crucifixion on one of the medals hinted at a penitential journey different from ours.

When we had performed our own brief ritual of veneration at the top of Mount Eagle by placing two fists of quartz on the cairn, it was a short stroll across to Lough Doo, which earns its name for darkness because it is slung low in the saddle between Mount Eagle and the Top of Leana. We followed the small trickle of water running out of this lough into the forestry of Glen Augh, forming the start of the Srahrevagh River. The trickle became a small stream gaining volume and accelerating force as we went down, with pine and spruce closing in around us. A line of old marker posts leads through this firebreak to Jamesie's Well a few minutes farther down. The well is in fact a set of three springs within thirty metres of each other, pouring out of bedrock through soft, peaty ground under the trees; the water is renowned for its purity and is said to be effective in the treatment of kidney stones, ever since a local man, Jamesie McIntyre, passed a kidney stone after drinking the water. The water's curative properties are denied, however, to anyone who attempts to sell it; it may only be freely given by those who come up here to collect it. According to Michael Chambers, there is no saint's day or pattern associated with the well.

The lodgepole pine sheltering these springs is old by the standards of commercial forestry and does not appear to have performed well as a timber crop. Not far from there, we crossed a wet clearing where the trees were dwarfed owing to some deficiency in the ground: eight to twelve feet tall, barely an arm's thickness after perhaps thirty years, not enough to give a return to the forester. Just then, as we tiptoed across the plashy surface of sphagnum, an unusual hissing sounded from the depths of the grove, like a lesson in wilding: at least one jay was there, a dividend from the failure of commercial forestry at this spot.

A wide firebreak leads gradually downhill from the well to the start of the forestry track. At the end of the old plantation many pines have been blown down by high winds, but a few veterans manage to defy the elements and hold up their crowns. This is a good spot for crossbills: we saw a small flock crossing the path almost on cue and made a note of the number (seven) to put into the national database. From this point at the edge of the old plantation the track drops gradually along the southern flank of Glen Augh and reaches the Srahrevagh River, by now a babbling brook with its own history of pools and shallows extending through a tall grove of pines, spruce and larch. Not far below the three springs the river disappears into the forest and enters a deep gorge which now boasts some magnificent forestry trees; one group of Japanese larch overlooking the gorge is deeply festooned with piles of *Usnea* lichen, an indicator of excellent air quality. The river then meanders in easier loops for another mile, through recent birch and oak plantings, before it drops away again into a series of falls, known locally as The Lep or leap. The most dramatic of these is where the river pours into a deep, three-storey gorge hidden under a canopy of ancient oaks. Michael Chambers reports that the pool at the base of the fall is about five feet deep, ideal for swimming. This is the nearest thing the Nephins has to a tropical idyll where the fantasist can dream of swimming with a lover. The picturesque splendour of this place is belied by the name, Sraith Riabhach, where riabhach usually means gloomy, dismal or wretched.

Even the mildest of winter days, however, keeps such dreams at a distance. At the end of my January trek from Skerdagh and Glenlara into the Nephin Forest, the rain had cleared; I stopped at the bridge over the Srahrevagh River and swapped my heavy boots for light trainers. As there was no wind to shake raindrops off the trees, the bare alders and birch were glinting at the tip of each twig with a fresh raindrop. Despite the general gloom of the day, it was remarkable how each drop glittered in its own globe of light.

Observations such as these feel like tokens of complete solitude. At the same time, it struck me that what we refer to as the sterility of conifer plantations may be rooted in our own inability to look for meanings. It is rare to meet anyone on a winter walk in Glen Augh. Its scenes, its effects of weather and atmosphere, its wild creatures and plants are almost entirely unapproached by art, by the depictions of photography, drawing or words.

The Nephin Forest may have cancelled many old tales of settlement and habitat on the open bog, but its own story awaits the telling as the wilderness proceeds. That story, as reported with images and words, might answer some basic questions, such as we ask when we want someone to communicate an experience: what is it like? We need a primer for such queries about the unloved or ignored plants of the forest:

What is wet rhododendron in January like?

What are they like, those points of mint-green lichen on willow?

What are yellowish willow buds like?

What are the tender green fronds of spruce like?

Precisely what colour is that dense green of sixty-year-old lodgepole pine?

What colour, if not black, is the dark shade within the upper branches of the same tree?

How tall is a spruce at sixty years compared to a masted ship?

How is molinia in January different from molinia in October?

What are they like, the dew-points on sphagnum shoots?

By comparison with the alien trees of this forest, so much of our natural world is already pre-wrapped in old symbolism and recognitions. Oak has a cultural history that has been written many times. Roses have their own institutions and literary histories: T.S. Eliot's roses in 'Burnt Norton' 'Had the look of flowers that are looked at.' Whereas our native plants, birds and animals are couched in patterns of recognition that have accumulated over centuries, a new landscape such as the Nephin Forest is a frontier for fresh meanings.

Snow at Altnabrocky

That first December snow was a blackness: hedges and trees lined in charcoal, crows having come into their own as lords of the place, grey cloud with a sooty core milling fine grains of snow to darken the shadows under hawthorn and escallonia. Everywhere, snow was failing to hold; it fell from wet, shiny branches and gave way to fine, bare silhouettes.

Things that used to find their own way – sheep in fields, thrushes in corners – were distraught; they would explode in a kind of denial out of their hiding places and be reduced to wandering the roads.

This snow blankets nothing. Nothing sleeps underneath. Everything is etched clearly in its blackness, like the inked lines of a plate for engraving. Snow is an easel for a canvas of darkness.

We had watched a pale hydrangea for months, enduring through autumn: now it is crushed by a havoc, collapsed by a greeting it could not endure; what had been nostalgia for summer is over now: our vigil has been clarified into a dead time where we have to survive, and wish for spring.

This betrayal turns us back indoors to our adequacies as we knock snow off our boots at the door. The boxed set. Tea and pies. Warm chores. The time we spend outside just enough to confirm us in the certainty that we do not belong there. We look through the glass at a robin as if it were a primitive fish in an ancient fossil, swimming through a remote stone, aeons away.

That would all be forgotten in turn: by late January, there's a growing checklist of signs of life to come: leafy shoots of honeysuckle in a sheltered culvert; a flowering blush of Irish heather (*Erica erigena*) now in its prime around

Lough Furnace; daffodils preparing their yellow brollies for an imminent opening; pale-green early leaves of montbretia like the brush strokes of a watercolourist working at speed; bluebell leaves in little sword clusters under the garden hazels; a crossbill singing from the top of a poplar in Glenlara while its mate on a lower branch gathers lichen for a nest; a raven in Glen Augh with a bunch of fleece in its beak; hanging tassels of hazel catkins teaching a lesson in gravity, something forgotten most days in the rush of wind and stirring treetops.

Then the quest for spring is suspended, giving way to more cold, and a hope of snow on the hilltops, of winter in its full array, like at Davos in Switzerland where the world élite met this week – those who were not too busy at home dealing with crises. Deep snow, like cake icing piled on slopes and rooftops; sound-muffling, breath-smoking snow being packed underfoot with every step; and with it, a vast blue light that gives you a headache if you forget to wear sunglasses; the kind of silence at altitude that D.H. Lawrence celebrated as an abstraction, where we are removed from mundane relations. This otherworld turns us into snow hunters.

Yesterday we went to Mount Eagle on a walk planned a few days earlier when there were forecasts of snow: in the event, the light covering that had fallen two nights previously was a thin gauze on the mountaintops, and even that was being hidden by rain clouds. Between Gogín and Mount Eagle I looked for the religious medals we had found earlier, but the ground was spotted with glistening medallions of melting snow, each of them resembling that little cellophane packet, so the search was hopeless. We stood in the drizzle on the top of Mount Eagle as Michael Chambers told the story of the IRA company moving across these hills after the engagement at Skerdagh. Two of us went to the falls at Srahrevagh at the end of the walk to watch the yellowish water crashing into the gorge: snow's bounty translated for the rainforest at Srahrevagh.

More snow did come eventually; hesitantly at first, a thin sprinkling on the fields when we got up one morning, and a more emphatic coat of white on the hills. By afternoon, in the centre of Westport, there was no trace of that first visiting; instead, the light of a clear blue sky reflected off white painted buildings had a clarity about it, not yet the light of spring's return, rather, the focussed intensity of true winter. Then snow came back at dusk in large, fluffy flakes, the kind called bratóga in Donegal Irish. And with snow came a giddiness, a feeling of truancy when school and work may be suspended, and adults have a licence to play like children with snowballs, snowmen and toboggans. On a late afternoon visit to a friend's house, where snowdrops stood proud in the front garden as sentinels of this weather, we walked up to the hazel spinney to look at new shoots of bluebells and daffodils, and a flowering Cornelian cherry, but there was a sense that that precious growth was arrested for now: we walked back to the house on a crunchy coating of glassy snow.

The following day's precipitation fell as sleet at Fahy, carrying another promise of fresh snow on higher ground, and a forecast for clearing skies to follow. So on Friday morning I drove to Letterkeen (Leitir Caoin, smooth hillside) under bright skies into a world that had been newly minted, with the mountains white under an even covering of fresh snow down to about three hundred metres. At the far side of Lough Feeagh, the long ridge of Ben Gorm rose up into this purity, from its southern shoulder, Bun a' Sáil, to the peak at 582 metres. (I had tramped along this ridge one time, in fresh, dry snow, and picked up the track of a hare, which then came to a sudden end on the open slope. The powdery surface nearby was marked by large wing feathers: what bird was big enough to lift a hare: a great black-backed gull, an eagle?) I parked at Letterkeen, where the riverside has been newly planted with broadleaf trees, the six-foot-tall pale plastic sleeves evenly spaced in the glen like an art installation. The river flowed with urgency in an aftermath of meltwater: as it passed the old gravel quarry, low sunlight ran through the water, and did not glance off it, but lit the slightly tawny water body and made the whole flow seem viscous. As the track climbs out of the glen towards Correenmore, you hear the jostlings of two rivers: one coming from Lough Bunaveelagh (Bun an Mhíle, the end of the mile?), the other flowing out of the Nephin Forest to the north; they join here to form a fork, a gabhlán, which gives the area its name, anglicised as Gaulaun.

The road to Altnabrocky turns right at the junction under Correenmore. The brow of the hill overlooking this junction is rocky, and contains the caves where the IRA company spent the night after the Skerdagh engagement before they made it to safety in Glendahurk. We were guided here one Sunday in summer by Michael Chambers, who led a small group of us up the steep slope, stair-stepping through a deep growth of heather to the outcrop near the top. Michael did not know the location of these caves as a child: the secret was kept by his father and grandfather, who thought the caves might be needed again for some covert purpose; therefore he had to set out to find them on his own, which he eventually did, his curiosity guided there by a kestrel wheeling in the air above the rocks. I thought that my fear of the underland might again get the better of me, but I was curious to see at least the entrance to this rebel hideout. The approach involves some fine balancing on sharp boulders, where thriving masses of bilberry, heather and golden rod obscure leg-breaker gaps in the terrain – but the profusion of vegetation here was a delight. Jessica followed the others through a wigwam of leaning boulders into a narrow, shoulder-wide passage, which then turned left, forcing you to turn sideways to squeeze through into the chamber. I felt a sickening at the confinement, and a premonition of panic at the prospect of having to queue behind others to return. At that moment, a thought of love did its work: Jessica had gone in, and I thought, 'Half of me is already in there', so I followed, and reached the cramped shelter among the jumble of boulders. In the cold, damp interior people squatted like baboons on various angles of rock, trying to absorb the idea of fugitives waiting here before making a break for Glendahurk. Gleams of light reached corners of the interior, and I was shown one shaft of daylight low down, where an entrance gave another point of access. I took this as my escape route, and lay down on my belly, squirming feet first through a slot as narrow as a coffin, and got out. Relieved to be back on the lush, airy hillside, I waited for a few minutes until the others returned, chatting and joking casually, oblivious to my private triumph.

Leaving that high-summer memory behind, I continued north along the foot of the hill, through a newly felled plantation. Some freshly cut spruce logs were marked and stacked along the track, the largest of these forty-eight years old by my count of growth rings, the harvest of a planting about 1970. The view along here was not of a forest, but of devastation, a fresh havoc wrought by machinery, what the American writer Aldo Leopold called a 'stump desert'; the only hint of life was the call of a wren moving in the brash like a refugee. I found some consolation in the fact that a new view had been opened up – of the Holes River as it meandered under the big moraine of Gaulaun. There was also a bright lake, Loch Geal, spread on the top of this moraine, to draw the eye, along with a smaller patchwork of pools and lochán. In fact, Loch Geal and its hidden twin Loch Dubh both sit on the first surviving parcel of flow country in this area, a foretaste of the vaster stretches of flow to the north, between Keenagh and Bellacorick.

Where this recent clear-fell ends and the track re-enters the cold shadows of plantation, there's an old forestry hut, reputedly the occasional home of pine martens. I stepped into the derelict, gloomy interior where forestry workers used to drink tea in the early years, before takeaway coffees and well-heated vehicles made such shelters redundant. Nor could I find any sign of pine martens; instead, the floor was darkened with sheep droppings. The moment was really consecrate to the light that reigned in this sheltered lay-by. I hunkered down outside the door on an old tyre and relished the warming sun as a drift of steam rose from a moss-covered bank at the edge of the forest. Snowmelt on the tips of branches and grasses had turned to points of glinting light: in the different refractions of light, these sparkled yellow, green, blue or mauve; I was enthralled by one particularly intense droplet hanging under the seed head of a common rush, shifting through oranges, yellows, greens and blues as it glowed and pulsed across the prism of colour like a Christmas decoration.

Then the shape of a raptor flashing across the clearing made me jump up and search the space with binoculars, but the sparrowhawk or ghosthawk had vanished. I picked up my rucksack and carried on through the plantation where the shadowed track was cold and the snow still frozen. Here, as ever, a goldcrest's calls sawed obscurely at the silence.

At the end of this alley, the track enters a shallow valley whose sides are lined with old forestry trees. Here, the efficiency of plantations has yielded to the character of topography: stands of lodgepole pine holding out on a slope too difficult for modern machinery; deep ground cover of heather on a well-lit west-facing side. And the Shranawoad River (Sraith na bhFód, srah of the grassy turf) running through it all, a portion of its banks stabilised with dry stonework, which the track crosses on a solid concrete bridge. From here I got the first full view of Nephin Beg, a solid white pyramid dominating the horizon.

Like most of the mountains in the eponymous range, Nephin Beg hides away from the viewer or tourist. While the Reek presents itself clearly above the town of Westport, Nephin Beg requires some effort to approach, and its drama reveals itself reluctantly, in surprising or unpredictable stages. On this eastern side, Nephin Beg slopes down in four separate ridges or buttresses. The first two of these hold a deep glen, Coire na gCapall, the corrie of the horses, in their embrace. One afternoon, as I walked along this track, I heard a tremendous rushing noise, similar to an aircraft taking off; this sound of wind was on such a vast, grumbling scale, coming from the west, that I felt sure it was created by wind sweeping into this corrie, with the funnelling Venturi effect that you often get in mountain glens and passes. Like other high features of Nephin Beg, you cannot appreciate it from the lower road. Only the rich volume of one of its streams, An Fiodán Mór, tells you that there's a large stretch of territory above you.

For the walker on their way to Altnabrocky, Nephin Beg appears like a physical challenge, which you have to overcome. I knew that walking can move mountains; I had put many domineering peaks behind me, but still felt that balance of desire and awe as I thought about going that distance. At this stage of the trek, another feature focuses the mind: at the north-eastern end of Nephin Beg, nestled in a hollow under the spur of Cruach na gCon (peak of the dogs) and the forest edge, there's Loch na mBarún (lake of the baronies), where Erris, Tirawley and Burrishoole meet. This isolated, rarely visited lake is not visible from the track; to reach it you have to scramble up the slope at the edge of the forestry or follow the stream that drains it and shapes a picturesque tumble of rocks just as it comes down to the track.

I spent some time one winter afternoon following this little fiodán through its narrow glen to reach the lake, and I searched for signs of grouse in the deep heather growing on the slopes here, to no avail. As I got close to the lake, the stream hid itself in a narrow trench among tussocks of purple moor grass, and was reduced to a rocky, gurgling sound. Then the lake itself was there in its silence, slung between the open hillside and the veteran trees of an old plantation – pine and larch in reduced condition owing to the poverty of the ground. I stopped there to eat a sandwich and watch the lake surface swept by chasing breeze-waves; when these gave way to a stillness, trees and heather were reflected in a blurry, impressionistic sketch. At Loch na mBarún the forest fringes the lake respectfully, in Zen tranquillity, and does not crowd it out: its administrative significance as the meeting point of three baronies may have saved this lake from being completely swathed in conifers, which is the case for many of the lakes north of here.

Loch na mBarún was still a shining pitch in my memory as I moved along the lower track; it was there that I came across the first signs of red deer in the area: a set of big prints on a peaty track skirting the trees.

At this point, the track starts a gentle ascent towards the base of Cruach Buí, a modest hill just over 200 metres high. By now, having put Nephin Beg behind my left shoulder, I looked down on a fine sweep of forest in the hollow under Loch na mBarún. By some quirk of generosity, the planters had left wide breaks and openings in these sections, softening the impact of their commercial designs. The snow was now deeper, making a dry crunching sound under my footsteps; I had been following the marks of foxes and sheep all morning, and now at last there were also deer slots zigzagging across the shoe-deep drifts. In many parts of Ireland and Scotland red deer populations have reached troublesome levels, but in north Mayo these introduced animals are still a wonder.

The last two kilometres of this route are less varied than before: a relatively straight run through mature plantation. The townland name here is Tamhnach na nUltaigh, field of the Ulster people, a souvenir of the migration of people to this area in the 1790s following the Battle of the Diamond in Armagh. Coal tits and goldcrests were calling from the trees, and the white ground sparkled with stars.

My destination was the Altnabrocky shelter, an open-sided wooden hut that people from Mountaineering Ireland have provided for walkers along the Western Way. The shelter is a rare facility in the remote stretches of this long-distance trail. The name means 'rocky gorge of the badger', but where this gorge is would be difficult to decide. The river of that name begins its journey in these woods, then passes the eponymous lodge several kilometres farther north before continuing its journey across open bog to Bellacorick, where it joins with the Oweninny to form the Owenmore.

Altnabrocky is for me a placename that captures the wildness of this part of the Nephins. In May 2015, a group of three sea eagles, possibly a family group from the Kerry population, was seen in this area for a few days. The memory of their presence still lingers here above the lakes, forests and mountain corries. The track I was following is also a gateway to Corslieve, Dáithí Bán's mountain, and eventually the white summit put in an appearance, like the snout of a modern locomotive moving across the horizon in a gap between the pines.

I felt that I had demonstrated the adage that Corslieve is the most remote mountain in Ireland: having spent the morning putting Nephin Beg behind me, all I could do in the time I had left would be to pay homage to the white massif and the lunar remoteness of its cairn. A neat timber sign with 'SHELTER' in bright yellow lettering invites you to turn left off the track and guides you to the hut two hundred metres farther on. There in the snow, with its snow-covered roof and stained timberwork, the shelter looked like an Alpine postcard scene. A mailbox mounted on an inner wall contained a few provisions: matches to light a fire, some tinned fish, a bag of nuts; a journal for visitors hung on the opposite wall. I signed my name on St Bridget's Day, the second entry that year. Then I sat to eat a sandwich and watched small stirrings in the wayside heather as the accumulated snow melted; everywhere it was falling in soft collapses and patterings, releasing its weight from the tips of trees and plant stalks.

I kept going after that, curious to follow the track as far as the timber staircase the volunteers from Mountaineering

Ireland have installed to take walkers onto the slopes of Corslieve. The track here was colder than ever; snow had drifted to more than twenty centimetres and still draped the young pines. I was in the cold lee of the mountain, on a disintegrating, flooded track, and felt a tiny aftermath of the same sunless shadow that had favoured the build-up of ice on the eastern flank of Corslieve thousands of years ago, when its great series of corries was sculpted by glaciers. After a final, tantalising sweep of the mountain with binoculars, and a fix on the distinct prominence of its cairn, it was time to turn back, and as I did I felt the despondency that sweeps over the walker, knowing that a circular route is impossible and that you have to retrace your footsteps. I went past the hut, trying to focus my mind on the mere action of walking, to put down the distance, but as I did so, the sky darkened, a shower of sleet came on like grains of thrown sugar, and a wind stirred, like a sign of disapproval from the forest.

A homeward route, though, is not simply an action rewind of the outward journey: there are changes in perspective, in weather, and in light, as well as the inner workings of fatigue. As I came back to the valley bottom between Loch na mBarún and Cruach Buí, I spotted a hind, or female red deer, on the southern slope of the hill, staring at me. If she did not start in terror like an experienced stag, she was on her guard on the open hillside as I crept along the track, shielded by a high bank. I fixed her again in the binoculars and then saw four more deer browsing in young plantation a little farther along the slope. The low evening light giving a gingery blush to the hillside was a fulfilment of the yellow in the name, Cruach Buí. Deer such as these had been hunted persistently that winter, but now in the evening light they were browsing in respite, with a hind keeping watch. As the light softened towards sunset, old stalks of molinia dissolved into a low mist across the levels. The track disappeared into another stand of tall trees, and by the time I had come through them, the sun had been succeeded by civil twilight, with its pinkish banner, the belt of Venus, wrapping the lower sky. The long ridge of Birreencorragh shaped the horizon to the south-east: in the blush of evening its white was intensified, as if the whole mountain – not just a thin, ephemeral, reflective covering – were composed of this substance, like the fine clay that potters work for porcelain.

A single kestrel, evidently the bird I had glimpsed earlier, crossed the clearing at the forestry hut and perched at the tip of an isolated spruce that had been spared by the felling. Its deep buff plumage glowed with the last remnants of daylight, and the bird stayed in that position as I went past towards Correenmore, the hill lying parallel to the track like a long-eared basset hound stretched forward on its belly, with its head pointing north.

I had not seen anyone all day, but now the evening brought a few arrivals, as if man, like the foxes, martens and otters, were a nocturnal dweller in these places: a red van came past me on its way out, another car with full headlamps came up the track along the river, carrying two friends of mine and their German shepherds. The excited barking of the big dogs about to be given their evening run echoed in the canopy of pines like a memory of wolves. And, as I reached the car park, another car was pulling out, carrying a courting couple.

The forestry track continues north past the Altnabrocky shelter for over four kilometres as far as Altnabrocky Lodge. The forest is old plantation on what used to be flow country, before the rich landscape of lochs and locháns was lost to the growth of trees: most of these stretches of open wastes are now scarcely accessible; instead, they work on the imagination from the map, a scattering of blue Wedgewood smithereens on the green plantation. The larger lakes have traditional names, Loch Geal, Loch Dubh, Loch na mBroc, which the cartographer Barry Dalby has recently salvaged from local memory, along with names for the hidden streams that now run deep in the forest: Fiodán Glan (clear stream), Gabhlán Marbh (dead junction) and Fiodán Damhán (stream of the young bull). Occasionally, a trout angler ventures in here during the summer; a young woman from Sweden camped here on her own a few summers ago and left her story in local memory without a trace of her name; I'd heard of an osprey seen here once on autumn passage.

I had plans to emulate that nameless Swedish visitor and camp in the forest, in an attempt to explore the open country to the north. In the event, Storm Eric put paid to those ambitions, but not before I had contacted two people who run a guiding business in Newport and spoken to them about my interests.

Ged Dowling and Georgia MacMillan are both graduates of the Outdoor Education Programme at GMIT in Castlebar who have made their home in Newport at the edge of the Nephin Beg Mountains. Their passion for exploring and walking drives their business, Terra Firma Ireland; Georgia has also spearheaded the Mayo Dark Skies Project within the Wild Nephin National Park. In the absence of artificial lighting across much of the Wild Nephin area, the night skies here are famous for their clarity when weather conditions permit. Georgia's Dark Skies Project involves an ongoing survey of light pollution and an awareness campaign – and has led to an annual festival, regular astronomy talks, and night excursions to watch the sky.

I linked up with them one afternoon in early February when the air was still truculent following rain overnight, and a gale was blowing some lingering scraps of showers off Clew Bay. We drove north into the forest at Letterkeen and surveyed again the devastation of recent clear-felling. The storm had put more water into the river at Letterkeen than I had ever seen. It was still boiling angrily over the weirs.

The track took us through this no man's land, then past the Altnabrocky shelter and on to forested lake country. A detour along the track towards the eastern townland of Tubbrid (Tiobraid, a spring) brought us to the shore of Loch Geal, the biggest lake in the area, a peaty shimmer of desertion in the shelter of veteran pines. Nearly a kilometre farther on, a smaller lake was crowded at the margin with a thick hoar of *Usnea* lichens on larches. With excitement, we jumped out of the car at this point, talking about the place's potential for wild camping – 'before the midges arrive,' I added.

The north-bound track through this stretch of forest passes some very poor stands of pine, which have been smashed and toppled by storms; the remaining trees are gaunt, crippled versions of the commercial norm, but even this wreckage has a value: here I heard the throaty drawl of a rutting stag in the autumn, mistaking it at first for the noise of a chainsaw. Hunters and their vehicles would scarcely be tempted into this obstacle course of fallen logs and brash.

Our drive came to a halt at a locked forestry gate. Once we stepped out of the car and went round the yellow barrier we faced the vastness of open bog stretching away to the horizon – over twenty-five kilometres of giddying space from here to Belderg on the north coast. This was what Praeger meant by a landscape that was 'almost frightening in its isolation'; as our approach was still under the sway of Storm Eric, we had no leisure to consider Praeger's high-summer scenery and dashed across to take a look instead at Altnabrocky Lodge.

The scale of the building surprised us: the original two-storey house in a plain early-Victorian design had been added to with a lateral extension along the same frontage. The downstairs windows of the older part were shaded by a roof canopy, with a large rack on the outside wall for fishing rods: with the river so close, you leave your rod set up at the house and walk directly to the beat. Despite vacancy, the building was well maintained in readiness for the coming fishing season.

This is one of many sporting lodges that are dotted across the remote river valleys of north Mayo. It dates from the 1840s – when Griffith valued it at £2 – and belonged for many years to the earls of Malahide Castle. During the Second World War, when there were fears for national treasures with the risk of bombardment, the main manuscript collection of the Irish Folklore Commission was moved to the lodge in 1940, where it remained for nine years. The Commission's Director, James Hamilton Delargy or Séamus Ó Duilearga, was obliged to make regular trips to Altnabrocky in order to check on the security of the collection and to consult with collectors active in Mayo at that time. These trips, from Dublin to the west by train, also involved arduous onward journeys by bicycle, as Delargy noted in his diary for 24th April 1944: 'Left Dublin 10 a.m. on the first of the bi-weekly trains to West. Very few people on train. Cycled Ballina to (Altnabrocky) Lodge… Wind against me from Crossmolina.'[42]

The building now serves as an angling lodge during the summer, when sea trout and salmon find their way here from Blacksod Bay via the Owenmore. Like others of its kind, Altnabrocky Lodge is a Victorian outpost, which still acts as a summer pied-à-terre for an élite and where an older pattern of deference and division is still discernible. Although the achievements of an independent, post-colonial nation may have bypassed the archaic calm of such a retreat, there is a different dynamic obtaining here – between wilderness and civilisation. A couple of cottages and outhouses from later periods attest to the fragility of human endeavours in the teeth of gales that whip down from the mountains and seethe through the ailing forests. That other element, water, is also a threat, eroding riverbanks and foundations, undermining roads and leaking through buildings.

A few plastic buckets we could see placed in the middle of the parlour floor witnessed this struggle at Altnabrocky. The river of the same name, which gives the lodge its meaning now that grouse shooting is a thing of the past, was a full-bodied pulse of current in its bending course near the house: come spring and summer this spate stream would again be the setting for sporting stories, that blend of nostalgia and renewal which spreads its anecdotes across streams and pools, despite declining fish populations.

Quickened by a mild feeling of trespass, we peered through windows at the quiet abandonment of a summer house and then staggered across a patch of sodden ground to reach a footbridge over the river where Ged and Georgia took a few photographs. Then Ged led us across two nearby fields – another plashy stagger – to the mound of an old ring fort, where we disturbed a group of sheep sheltering under a grove of silvery rowans. Antiquity was a less enticing lesson than the basic principles of cold and exposure that day, and the frailty of our efforts to tame the elements. The booming susurration of the forests seemed laden with warnings about climate change, as many trees were no longer a match for the rigours of that place, and were gradually giving way.

After that unplanned trip, when I got home I fell asleep on the sofa and had a brief dream about wilderness inspired by the isolation and desertion of the Lodge. The dream pictured a high escarpment of rock, with a shattered plateau rather like a stage platform, all of it in the swirl of stormy weather. I saw it from the point of view of someone in a crowd at an open-air concert. Flood waters were rising on either side. Then a red deer stag with full antlers appeared at the top of the cliff and as it did, the flood came washing across the upper level. I woke just as the whole scene, including the animal, was engulfed by rising water. The image was the very essence of wildness, where a theatre of elements overwhelms the object, so that there is nothing left to contemplate.

The stag in my dream was a familiar symbol of the romantic imagination and it may have come from seeing Landseer's famous picture 'Monarch of the Glen' in Edinburgh the previous summer. Antlered red deer as a token of wildness and otherness were commonplace in

Victorian Scotland and Ireland, and were still used as a promotional signpost in Donegal and Killarney. But the image of the overwhelming flood and the destructive power of natural elements sprang from different associations in my mind. These were connected principally to one key writer in Irish tradition, the diarist Amhlaoibh Ó Súileabháin (1783-1838), in whom we can trace a unique awareness of the natural world. For anyone wrestling with ideas of wilderness and the wild in Ireland, I believe that Ó Súileabháin is a key witness, and his position as a mediator between cultures is unique. Although he had no direct contact with the area of my study, his diary and other writings were constantly on my mind, and my dream after-image of the visit to Altnabrocky came directly from him. Sooner or later he was bound to find his way into this report.

Amhlaoibh Ó Súileabháin was a native Irish speaker from the Killarney area, whose family migrated to Waterford in 1789 when he was little. His father, a hedge school teacher, eventually settled near Callan, Co. Kilkenny, where he educated two of his sons to follow their father's profession. After the death of his father, Amhlaoibh continued teaching pupils at his school in Callan, and also opened a shop, leased farmland, and dealt in livestock. In 1827, he began to write a cinnlae or diary in Irish, where he made regular observations on the countryside around him. As a teacher, farmer, and businessman, he had interests across wide fields of enquiry and his diary is a rich store of contemporary language. A casual inventory of his interests would include: weather patterns; aspects of scenery; agricultural markets; seasonal cycles of flowering plants and migratory birds; the calendar of religious and native feast days; the farming year; contemporary disputes about tithes; local crimes and legal cases; the progress of the Irish cholera outbreak of 1832 to 1833; current affairs (including wars in Europe); his wife's fatal illness; trips to Dublin to buy stock for his shop; the etymology of Irish words; visits to neighbours; walks in the countryside with friends and acquaintances.

The *Cinnlae* is greatly prized as a record of country life in pre-Famine Ireland, but as an early, proto-scientific nature record it is unique. Even through the blur of Ó Súileabháin's highly irregular Irish usage we get a detailed vocabulary for plants and animals, while the writer teases out the separation between species. He knows that barn swallows and swifts are different species, and that the latter arrive in spring a couple of weeks after the former. These birds, he explains, 'leave us in flocks for Africa; and then return to us in spring.' In August 1828, he observes of swallows, 'Very soon they will be leaving this land. They are along the sea coast in flocks or groups, ready to go across the Irish Sea.'[43] Fieldfares, he correctly surmises, are also migratory, though he does not know where the cuckoo, the quail and the corncrake spend the winter. His diary carefully records dates of arrival and departure of migratory species, along with patterns of their singing and calling. He delights in the summer visitors, setting down versions of their calls: the quail 'ag fuid fuide,' the corncrake 'ag aic aic,' 'agus an cuach ag cuachaireacht'; and he is disconsolate when they have left. In his analysis of the names of flowers, as well as trying to sort out some confusion in the application of vernacular names, he coins new Irish terms for botanical science, trying to translate concepts from the system of classification devised by the Swedish authority, Linnaeus, who invented the scientific naming we use today. The meadow saffron (*Colchicum autumnale*) he says is plentiful near Callan, a 'rather unusual flower… of the hexandrian class [den treibh seisir], and of the tregynian kind [den ord tríbhean].'[44]

In this area, as well as in his observations about meteorology and current affairs, we see an educated man with cultural links to cosmopolitan Europe translating ideas and practices into his Irish vernacular. This is especially remarkable as Ó Súileabháin wrote without any thought or prospect of publication at a time when Irish literature circulated in a manuscript *samizdat* and when the Irish vernacular lacked the authority of an academic standard. The linguistic usage of the diary, therefore, is highly irregular, and seems in its phonetic variation more attuned to an oral tradition than to a written context. At the same time, because it was directed to empirical details of nature and rural life, and used none of the conventional patterns of literary forms, the *Cinnlae* is a rich repository of the Irish language predating the main period of the Gaelic Revival by several decades.

While the *Cinnlae* is his main achievement, Ó Súileabháin was not only an empirical writer: there is, through the manuscripts, a scattered legacy of poems, and an intriguing set of stories and sketches concerning the deeds and adventures of an heroic figure called Calmar. Calmar is identified several times as one of the O'Tooles, a rebel clan from Wicklow, but elsewhere he is given the surname Mac Mearchuradh, or son of Mercury. This identification with Mercury/Hermes, the messenger god of classical tradition, is underlined when he guides Calmar to a house for shelter and Calmar notices a scent of flowers left when the god vanishes as suddenly as he appeared; this is a clear borrowing from Homeric tradition, where Hermes gives moly, a medicinal plant, to Odysseus in order to cure his men from the spells of the enchantress Circe. In another fragment, a rainbow heralds his appearance, placing him on a par with Iris, the other classical messenger. These identifications with classical tradition are clues to the wider culture Ó Súileabháin drew upon as he wrote these adventure sketches and stories.

Calmar's life is a broad historical allegory of Ireland's relations with England. His father and uncle are said to have fought on the Jacobite side in the Williamite wars, but managed to hold on to his ancestral property through 'King William's guarantee'. This allows Calmar to grow up as the son of a prosperous farmer, and to travel to France every year to visit his exiled uncle and to study. When at home, according to another fragment, he manages to live the life of a benign aristocrat: 'do chaith a aimsir le fiadhach, le sealgaireacht, ag éisteacht le gearánaibh a scológ agus a lucht oibre; he passed his time hunting, fowling, listening to the complaints of his tenants and of his employees'.[45] With Calmar styled, not as a peasant, but as a son of genteel upbringing, he becomes compatible with the heroic protagonists of contemporary literature. By a manipulation of chronology, ('I was not born for a considerable time after these events,' he tells his hosts), Calmar comes to maturity at some time in the early nineteenth century, following war between revolutionary France and England, when there were new hopes of freedom in the struggle with English power in Ireland.

In the most sustained and coherent of the stories, 'The Pursuit of Calmar', the hero travels from the east of Ireland to the author's birthplace in the Kerry mountains, where he meets the O'Neill, who has been driven into western exile with his family. Following a number of tests of character in wild settings, Calmar is received into the family, where he meets, and eventually falls in love with O'Neill's daughter, the Beauteous Maiden, Ainnir Álainn. O'Neill reminisces with Calmar about their exploits during the recent rebellion in 1798 and recognises him as a scion of the rebellious O'Tooles. With their bond confirmed, Calmar spends time enjoying the hospitality of O'Neill's western home. Then, following a hunting accident, the hero is attacked and killed by an English group, who in turn are slaughtered by O'Neill's men. Ainnir Álainn is overtaken with grief at the death of Calmar and dies a year later.

Many elements of this story are taken from Lady Morgan's novel *The Wild Irish Girl* (1806): the exiled chieftain living in a western wilderness, his beautiful daughter in love with the visiting hero, the family's situation an improbable blend of penury and prestige. Ó Súileabháin's story is too short, the transitions too sudden, and the characters too functional for us to keep disbelief suspended; instead, what is of outstanding interest here, even within the limited format, is Ó Súileabháin's handling of setting, including landscapes, weather and dwellings.

Wild weather and dereliction are almost constant features of the landscapes that Calmar explores on his journeys. The old hermit he meets in the monastery at Kells lives in a ruin, 'na ceillighe dá leigeann chun fiadhantais'; in his pursuit of this old man, Calmar enters a lonely tower by a Gothic doorway, and when he finally catches up with him, he is told that Ireland is exposed to wild conditions, and that the dispossessed are cast out onto a landscape of harsh elements: 'Frost-abounding, deep-ravined, rocky mountains afford us no protection; neither do awesome, gloomy caves, nor dark lonely woods.'[46] Wildness becomes the essential condition of Ireland, and the west of Ireland becomes its 'classic ground', as Horatio puts it in Lady Morgan's novel.

Following the hermit's advice, Calmar journeys westward, via the Rock of Cashel, and reaches Ó Súileabháin's ancestral homeland among the Kerry mountains. He is constantly exposed to an array of disturbances, of weather and terrain, but like the typical questing hero of tradition, he survives various ordeals – including a brief night in an enchanted house, where forces of good and evil fight through the haunted night. While Calmar is the protagonist of a staunchly national tale, the pageantry and effects of his journey are drawn from the romantic literary mainstream, with towering cliffs, ancient oaks, steep cataracts and high mountains. At the very limit of his resilience, when his world has been shaken by 'wild formlessness', his situation is relieved when he discovers the dwelling of the exiled O'Neill. At first it appears like a miserable hovel in a grotto, but when Calmar is eventually welcomed by the chieftain and his retainers, they pass through the grotto, via 'a narrow, crooked, pitchdark recess, through the very middle of the hill right through to the other side' [135], where he enters a kind of Gaelic Arcadia.

> They saw the sun shining; alternate showers and sunshine ripening every fruit of the earth it is possible for the human mind to think of; streamlets babbling through the valleys, as if loath to leave this earthly paradise, presently leaping noisily from cliff to cliff, and then wending their shrunken ways through mountains, till they are merged in the soulless sea; heavy-headed wheat on one side, khaki-coloured barley on the other, oats in this wild glen, rye in yon field, an ozier plantation on a cliff side: a nimble-tailed lamb sucking its

mother, a foal itching the mare, a sire-horse neighing in the water meadow.[47]

Other details from this idyll add more local detail, with a description of 'cool pools' where Calmar swam to refresh himself: these were 'screened off from one another by hedges of thorny holly, that leader of the wood, by wild and fragrant sweet-briar, by weakly woodbine, stern black-thorn, hazel, the tree of love, and by all other fragrant and beautiful shrubs.' [137] Following his swim in the pools, Calmar is 'clothed in garments of finest texture and beauty' and then joins O'Neill and his family in the shade of oak trees for a banquet. In this idealised, Homeric setting of welcome and storytelling, O'Neill still reiterates the trope of wilderness, as though it underscored Irish dispossession. He has been obliged to sell his estate and come to this desert fastness – 'Dob eigin dom teacht don ionad fásamhail seo'; despite this alienation in his own land, the writer's fantasy still confers prestige and style – even opulence – on the exiled chieftain. By a similar uneasy balance, in a later sketch, we are told that Calmar's father manages to 'keep open house for his farmers, for their families, and for everybody. He [also] kept a pack of stag hounds and some splendid horses. Great though his means were, he was living from hand to mouth.'[48]

Other stories in the Calmar cycle repeat the motifs of wildness and remote houses, as well as adventure with an aristocratic family, though the setting is now removed to Ó Súileabháin's adopted south-east, the landscape recorded by the *Cinnlae*. The extremes of weather and terrain where Calmar's heroic prowess is demonstrated are heavily flavoured by romantic writing and iconography. In a repeat of the O'Neill episode, Calmar meets and befriends another family, including Diarmaid Donn and his sister Ainnir Álainn. His qualities are again demonstrated after a great storm, when the whole land is flooded, and the river Nore 'froths and foams through, tumbling over cascades, reeling, tearing away banks'. Whole cottages and lands along the river are being overwhelmed, including a bridge where Ainnir Álainn had been standing. On seeing her figure being swept away in the brew of foaming water, 'With a bound he plunges into the rapid uproarious flood' and rescues her, 'with his noble breast, cleaving the massive, deep-sounding, white-foamed, hungry swirling waves till in triumph he reached dry land with his precious burden.' Following frantic efforts, they manage to resuscitate this wild Irish girl and present her to Calmar. He has by now fallen in love with this aisling or dream-woman, who now appears in a different imaginative guise, as one of the three graces of pastoral tradition.

The final sketch with Calmar, 'Lá ar na Bántaibh/A Day in the Meadows', includes a superb piece of romantic scene-setting. Calmar finds Ainnir Álainn tending to her sheep and rescuing a young lamb, just as he had rescued her from the river in spate. The atmosphere is gentle, nature is benign: it is May, and 'The noble lark sang unceasingly for them in the heights of heaven.' The earlier power of the flood had torn two huge oaks from the riverbanks, so that they lay across each other, forming a 'sylvan bridge', 'an enormously high and airy bridge of broad-leaved brown oak'. From this vantage point the two lovers survey the landscape of the south-east, its woodland, crops and castles. The passage is Amhlaoibh Ó Súileabháin's hymn of praise to his adopted area, though not without a patriotic frown at the history of conquest, evident in the Norman castle they can see: 'Nach láidir é an bádhbhdhún, nach doimhin an cladh mór agus é ar na líonadh ag uisce na Craosóige; how strong the bawn is; how deep the great fosse when filled by the water of the Craosogue!'[49]

These Calmar stories are sketches only, as if a longer work was envisaged, but given the limited context in which the writer was working, in a language without an infrastructure of publishing, they were probably never destined to be anything more. There is a poignancy in the author's creation of an heroic avatar, in which he, a busy schoolteacher and businessman, projects a fantastic version of himself as a hero wandering through an idealised landscape. Ó Súileabháin has no interest in what we would call characterisation, and so his Calmar is little more than a function, a kind of iconic Wilhelm Meister on a journey through a landscape of significant forms. But as exemplars of tradition, the sketches are extremely interesting, where a writer with stylistic habits formed in Irish literature creates scenes and narratives blending ancient classical lore with recent romantic taste for wild scenery. There is also a strong Gothic ingredient in the ruined monasteries and labyrinthine fastnesses visited by Calmar; in fact, the adjective 'Gotamhail', which is repeatedly applied to ruined structures, serves as a signpost to a literary genre that was well represented in the chapbooks and piracies of hedge-school reading. According to Antonia Mac Manus, in her fascinating book, *The Irish Hedge School and its Books 1695-1831*, 'Irish readers welcomed the rebellious Gothic literature, which peaked as Ireland was making preparations for the revolution of 1798.'[50] Her summary of the Gothic genre, as represented in the works of Walpole, Reeve and Radcliffe, applies perfectly to the conventions of the Calmar stories: 'Scenes of danger, fear, imprisonment or torture took place in sublime settings such as mountains with rocky crags and deep gorges, or dark underground places calculated to stimulate the emotion of terror, while normal social life continued in beautiful villas, gardens and vineyards.'⁵¹ This very contemporary literary taste shows how much the hedge school was part of a cosmopolitan literary culture, supported by a thriving printing industry, as Mac Manus has shown. Ó Súileabháin himself is an example of how readily people can be fully attuned to the culture of a metropolitan centre, even where their language and location would appear to put them away out on the margin. The moment is captured perfectly by Lady Morgan in *The Wild Irish Girl*, when the English hero Horatio blunders into the private quarters of the heroine Glorvina, to discover a room full of periodicals and magazines befitting a London salon, as if this remote western castle housed a Regency boudoir. Glorvina's bookshelves were 'filled with the best French, English, and Italian poets' and, to Horatio's utter astonishment, not only some new publications scarce six months old, but two London newspapers of no distant date, lay scattered on the table.'⁵² The imaginary moment in Lady Morgan is paralleled in Ó Súileabháin's creation of a romantic avatar, and both reveal the limitations of later nationalist attempts at constructing a myth of cultural purity in the wilder regions of Ireland.

The civilised culture of the writer is pitted, in the Calmar stories, against the rigours of the Irish weather and western Irish terrain. While the literary conventions of the romantic sublime and its Gothic offshoot are used to set a protagonist against a backdrop of terrible storms and floods, there is also a persuasive sense of realism in the accounts of raw elements and terrible weather threatening the meagre shelters of the dispossessed. In fact, at one moment in 'The Pursuit of Calmar', the hero contemplates a monstrous darkness, 'The night lay heavy, dark and repellent on the face of the heights, on the peaks of the higher hills and on the flanks of the mountains. A mourning veil is unfolded on the face of the skies and the stout hero could not see the length of his hand.' In this condition of complete exclusion from his environment, Calmar thinks, 'I am now like one before the creation of the world, before were created the twinkling stars, or the cheerful moon, or the resplendent, gaseous sun, what time each element was as yet blurred and indeterminate, warring with the others, until the Spirit of the Creator brooded over them, turning them towards seemliness and order.'[53]

Here, as elsewhere, a kind of cosmic disorder threatens, until the idea of God intervenes as a force of control. In the western Arcadia of his hosts, the benign natural order is underwritten by pious observance and prayer; otherwise, the universe would be overwhelmed by a chronic threat of wild terrain and weather. In 'The Ruin of the Forty Shilling Freeholders', a deliberately topical tale, a dispossessed family are afforded hospitality by Calmar's hosts, and are saved from the terrible rigours of the environment outdoors: 'A storm raged from the east, swaying the sturdy leafless oak from top to bottom. The staunch ash-tree quaked for fear of the dreadful storm. The blood-thirsty eagle screamed from the cliff. A pack of savage wolves howled in the desert.'[54] These dramas of wild weather are a testing ground for heroism and a backdrop to Gaelic civilisation, but they also take on a new colour for us as modern readers, faced with the unsettling weather patterns of climate change. And we don't, yet, know if our science and politics will work successfully together to save us from this catastrophe, as Catholic piety and Gaelic civilisation operated in O'Neill's western Arcadia as principles of security and order in a wilderness.

Two days later, having shelved my camping plans because of the weather, Ged and I set off again to explore the area to the north of the lodge. Our intention was to walk a section of forest west of the lodge and then, following a firebreak through the plantation, to explore the flow country in the townlands of Muingaghel (Moing an Ghaill, mossy fen of the foreigner) and Uggool (Ogúl, a hollow), ending up at the main road near Ballymunnelly. In the bright, newly washed allowance of that morning, Corslieve and its corries were majestic in the distance to the west, with a scattering of fresh hailstones added to the remnant of snow. The world felt scoured clean by the brisk discipline of winter and was letting in some sunlight under a lid of cloud: this in turn was extinguished by the pattering grain of more hail showers.

The route we planned was a proposed new route for the long-distance Western Way, which currently takes pedestrians onto the main road for several kilometres near Bellacorick. We had studied these plans in the consultants' report, but we never found the gap in the forest and instead had to take a long detour up the slope towards Corslieve to get round the treeline. Ged checked elevations and distances on the digital map he carried on his smartphone app; my older custom of consulting a printed map was not needed that day, and my OS sheet stayed in the bag.

As we ascended the long, heathery ramp of a firebreak towards Corslieve, the views to the north and east opened up: forest, moraine and flow stretching away in the bruised light of squall-bearing clouds. This is heavily glaciated country, with a series of corries along the eastern foot of the mountain, and more pockets to the north, where lakes shimmer in the ditches created by moraines. The long whaleback of Corslieve marks the edge of the ice sheet: ice and snow built up on the eastern lee of the mountain, forming glaciers moving east and north; by contrast, the ground to the west has none of the grandeur of the ice-worn, east-facing corries overlooking Altnabrocky: the largest of these, Coire na nGarú, was a towering dark wall in the flank of the mountain that morning.

As we came round the top of the plantation at about 300 metres and got our first look at the Waterfall Stream, we saw two sheepmen and a red quad on the slope below us rounding up a few animals; then another hefty shower of hail whipped into us, sending the two men home with their flock. I tightened the fastening on my hood to save my face from the needle points of hail, and could look no more look on the world than a Muslim woman in her niqab. We crept down towards the stream in a fierce crosswind. As the ground bottomed out, the hail passed and we could relish the spot our detour had brought us to: a wide, shallow bowl of heather crossed by a pure, glassy, hearty stream flowing out of Loch na mBreac Caoch, another lake of one-eyed trout.

The stream then quickened its pace, tumbling into the deep-grown sides of an allt, where its water foamed and fizzed with the greenish tinge of champagne: after a few turns it then went straight, pouring over the lip of a low sill, and then fell off the edge into a pool twenty feet down, a broad sheet of cataract like the bridal train of a goddess on her way up the mountain for a ceremony. This deep gorge with lush heather obscuring the track was not without its dangers, so we carefully rounded the bluff above the waterfall and came down. This wonderful stream then flows

across the open bog and skirts the plantation line in a slower
tempo under a new name, the Owenlusky (Abhainn
Loiscthe, parched stream, so called presumably because of
the proximity of lakes that do not supply it with water,
giving the stream a deprived or parched appearance during
drought). We hunkered down here in the shelter of a peaty
bank to eat a sandwich.

Our afternoon's walk took us away from the Owenlusky
onto open flow country, the first I had walked for a long
time. We picked our way carefully among locháns, poking
at mossy puddles before venturing a step: Ged prodded at
one narrow trough of pale sphagnum several feet deep – a
simple plunge-trap like this, Ged explained, would be a
recipe for hypothermia on a winter's day, which is why a
licensed tour guide like himself has to carry an emergency
supply of dry clothing. The larger locháns were wide
enough for a brew of wind and waves: a feeding frenzy of
angry water jostling at dark edges; some of them had high,
tufted little islands where heather proliferated in the
absence of grazing animals.

These patchworks of bog and open water make the flow
country a wonderland for the walker: when you view them
at first, they can appear featureless, but the lakes and
locháns of this terrain are often hidden a couple of feet
below their margin, and it is only as you walk into these
vast spaces that their features open up. In summer
especially, the grey-brown desert unfolds as a wonderland
of otter tracks, wader calls, and little river courses choked
with ferns and willows. These vast peatlands of north Mayo
have a different appeal from the scenic standards of
mountains and coast, but there is quality of light and space
in the flow that is unique.

A rough day in February curtails these perceptions, however. We marched on towards Ballymunnelly, which appeared in the distance as a quilt of green fields studded with bungalows. On our way there, we came to McAndrew's Stream, a surprise of new water we approached across an overlooking bluff. Another jostling gale with a freight of hail blew into us as we followed this stream down past the cropped lawns of the srah in the river's looping embrace. These grassy levels were littered with black erratics of peat and large baulks of pine – one of them bellied like a big seal – which the floods had undermined in the riverbank. We stopped to look at the lumpy traces of an old booley hut, where someone used to creep in under a low roof of bog deal and scraws to bivouac for a few hours during the short nights of summer.

By now we were almost off our feet in the blowing conditions and scurried along as far as a cottage ruin, where we could stand in the shelter of the gable. Ged telephoned Georgia to arrange our lift, then we carried on towards a high flood of winds in spruce trees around the farm. The red quad we had seen on the mountainside above the waterfall was parked in a concrete yard; sheep stood in a huddle in the shelter of an outhouse, like migrants in the hold of a boat. The farmer had retreated, and so we stepped over his gates, leaving mud from our boots on the rungs. He would know that someone had passed through the yard without asking.

From there, it was just over a kilometre as far as the Owenmore, a broad stream forming the northern border of Wild Nephin. We could see cars in the distance moving steadily along the main Castlebar to Belmullet road, signs of busy, modern life going on heedlessly, hermetically sealed from place and weather. The road brought us to a plain, modern bridge over the river, with wind humming in its bright aluminium rail. The passing traffic was now an audible hiss.

The broad, grey river running away under my feet already held a few early salmon that had come in from the winter sea. If they were spared capture by otters, anglers' rods, or poachers' nets, they would stay in this river until spawning time next December or January and not feed throughout all that time, relying on their body's reserves. At the same time as these early-run fish, the surviving salmon from this past winter's spawning were coming back down the river to the sea. These 'kelts' are lean, depleted fish, a starved version of the heavy spring fish they must encounter on their way down. And so, as one year ends in the salmon's life cycle, another begins with a few early springers, the scarce fish hunted by the anglers who brave these conditions.

For now, though, there were no anglers, and no signs of any fish in the grey waters: just one heron corkscrewing away above the trees, flying upstream.

Once you get back onto the road with speeding traffic, the spell of a walk is completely broken: discarded bottles and other rubbish littering the roadside are an insult to add to the buffetings of passing cars. This part of north Mayo is a post-industrial landscape of abandoned peat workings around Bord na Móna's old power plant: signs still warn the walker of the danger of deep water in old drainage ditches; wild-seeded lodgepole pines form a kind of feral scrub on bare, blackish stretches of old workings. There is no hint from here, as you walk the main road, of another wilderness of flow country stretching away to the north, once you get past the industrial junk of Bellacorick and its assertive new wind farm. That would be a journey for another day. For now it was a relief to see that one car slowed down as it approached us, and we clambered eagerly into the haven of Georgia's Toyota.

Coda: The Fairy Mound of Murrevagh

I have come to the machair at Murrevagh to mark the end of winter. Whatever the weather may yet do, there is more than enough in the hedgerows, woods and verges to say that spring is here and with it another growing season: the snowdrops are over, daffodils are in flower, and lesser celandines are thriving again, even where the banks have been sprayed with Roundup. I saw flowers on blackthorn and sallow this morning, telling me that bumblebees will soon be hovering among the pollen-rich stamens for their first feed of nectar.

The Irish name Muirbheach, meaning a sandy place, identifies Murrevagh as a long stretch of machair, dunes and beach in the top north-western corner of Clew Bay, with a small golf course at its northern end. Like many machair sites, it is heavily grazed commonage, where sheep and cattle pick a meagre sustenance throughout the year, and a few harebells and yellow bedstraw survive to remind you of the bygone glories of machair vegetation. With livestock occasionally straying onto the beach and leaving their droppings, the beach here does not qualify for Blue Flag designation, so this is still an 'unofficial' beach, without public toilets or lifeguards; to those who know about it, it's a favoured spot for swimming and walking away from the radar of approved designations. The regulatory presence of authority here is light: two lifebelts on posts in their yellow boxes; an occasional collection of bagged rubbish which local volunteers gather from the shoreline; a sign sponsored by a local multinational welcoming you to Murrevagh showing a herd of cattle lying on the beach in proud possession; another sign prohibiting vehicles on the machair

– though you can drive across the golf course, as I did, to get to a small gravelled car park.

The Scottish writer Kathleen Jamie observes that by the third week of February, 'one can say for sure that the light is back', a rubicon that works for me as I sit in my car in the warmth of sunlight and an unusually mild temperature in the mid-teens. At the same time, a vigorous breeze rocks the shell of the car to remind me of the bleakness and exposure that is usually the walker's lot at Murrevagh at this time of year. Canadian brent geese and great northern divers are still wintering along this shore; it will be weeks before the first wheatears arrive and little terns won't come through until May.

This winter has been remarkably mild, a knowledge that comes nowadays with a shadow of foreboding: is it global warming, or just the freak of a mild winter, that has put a burst of blackthorn blossom on so many hedgerows, and is already bringing hawthorn into leaf, greening the verges? For now, I am putting weather statistics to one side as this is a day for exploration, to be out, with binoculars and notebook, and a curiosity about one feature of this area I have yet to visit: Símurrevagh, a drumlin at the southern end of the machair where the good fairies of Murrevagh are supposed to reside. The drumlin is now linked to the machair by a stretch of saltmarsh, but it used to be an island at one time. The benign fairies mentioned in the placename are celebrated in a traditional rhyme:

Sídh Muirbhighe na dtonn
Sídh riamh nach ndearna feall
Sídh aoibhinn na mban fionn

which I translate loosely as follows:

Murrevagh fairies of the shore
Never harmed a living soul
Lovely fairies of the fair ones.[55]

In his 2012 classic *The Old Ways*, Robert Macfarlane describes sleeping outdoors at Chanctonbury Ring, an ancient ritual site in West Sussex, and being woken in the small hours by unearthly shrieks and screams. The experience was completely unexpected and clearly unsettled him. As he later discovered, the site has a long history of haunting and was reputedly a place where you could meet the Devil and barter your soul for a bowl of soup or porridge; for those who are interested in such things, Chanctonbury Ring ranks high in lists of haunted sites. Although a seasoned traveller of pragmatic Scottish heritage, Macfarlane made a connection between what Synge and Yeats would have called the 'psychic memory' of a place, and their own imaginings – if we discount the possibility that Macfarlane was the victim of an orchestrated hoax, or had been visited by a particularly noisy pair of barn owls.[56]

This connection to psychic memory is something I have wanted to test in a suitable location, and I have opted for Símurrevagh, where the fairies are reputed to be benign, so any anxieties I might have will be of my own making. Furthermore, there seems to be no better way to start the fine season than a bivvy in a sheltered hollow within earshot of the sea; I am also adapting Nan Shepherd's maxim that 'No one knows the mountain completely who has not slept on it',[57] and I suppose this must also be true of the coast, with its lunar and tidal acoustics.

I take my first load of gear from the car and set out along the exposed beach: after so much dry weather, there is not much fresh water leaking across the sand from the machair; the beach is an even khaki colour, with darker striations and ripplings of grey and brown. The sea itself is like cold, hammered foil, the 'intractable metal' of Sylvia Plath's poem 'Blackberrying'. In a warm country the scene would be otherwise, Venus-inviting – but no such love goddess will be born here today, even though the wind is almost warm, blowing a thin stream of sand grains across the flats.

A couple and their young boy, tiny figures in the landscape ahead – what future will there be for the child on our damaged planet?

At the end of the main beach, I come round the narrow marram-clad edge of machair where a massive storm some years ago sliced through the seaward slope, creating a cut-off outline, like a low escarpment. Then I am onto a smaller, narrower beach tilted gently towards the water like a car-testing track, with rocky, blackish shore outside it. Between the marram brow and the sand, there's a rough limestone shingle studded with large red-sandstone boulders. These were put here originally to protect the dunes from erosion, but subsequent storms have shifted them discreetly out of their line and worked them into random order on the pale-grey limestone with the art of a Japanese Zen gardener.

Where the sand of this beach comes to an end, the larger limestone blocks of the shore are like dinosaur eggs nestling against the artificial rampart of sandstone, forcing me to step up onto the sandy bluff. This lifts me up to a view of the next bay, a narrow, shallow rectangular kilometre of grey water much favoured by all three species of diver, great northern, black-throated and red-throated, those birds spending so much time in the water that medieval philosophers hesitated whether to classify them as birds or fish. The big rubble of this coast compels you back onto the soft machair, where, at this end, in a patchwork of pools and waterlogged trenches, it zones off into saltmarsh, such is the impact of seawater washing over it on high spring tides.

I marched across this exposed, brackish desertion on my way to the drumlin of Símurrevagh, and wondered where I might find shelter for a tent. Wind, water and cropping animals have scoured, eroded and worn everything down. Exposure was the basic condition of the place, hostile to my requirements. Even the pages of my notebook were jumping and flapping uncontrollably.

The drumlin is ringed by a dry-stone wall and an assertive sheep fence: the old wrought-iron gate between a railway sleeper and an ancient spar, amazingly, opened smoothly on a well-balanced hinge. The slope of pasture was cut across with low, eroded embankments; long sword-blade leaves of New Zealand flax formed crests along the tops of these banks, flapping like pennants in the breeze. One hollow contained the scattered debris of roof sheeting and six eight-foot timber posts where the farmer had ventured to build a shelter in the face of the pitiless Atlantic. A skylark pottered about on the top of one of these posts. If I were shipwrecked here, like Alexander Selkirk, I should be tempted to begin with this litter of salvage, and build my shelter with these galvanised sheets.

Once I got to the top, surrounded by a vigilante flock of sheep, I found hedges cowering low against the sea winds: the fields on the southern side were fully exposed to the westerlies, so I came back to the sandy lee of the hill and its furrowed slope, the remains of an old fort. I chose one hollow, between a line of New Zealand flax and a marram-grown bank, to pitch my tent. I thought of the dry, slapping blades of the flax as my night noise, and worried that they, rather than the fairies, might keep me awake.

This was a secure fort in ancient times: saltmarsh and rocky coast on the seaward side; on the other side a long, muddy inlet running up from the castle at Rosturk (Ros Toirc, headland of the boar). As I got set up, the tide was out, and the exposed mud of the inlet shimmered like a blade that had been sharpened by the brine's edge; this would be a perfect spot for curlews, greenshank, redshank, and other waders as the tidal waters pushed them in.

Within half an hour, my tent was pitched in the acrid atmosphere of sheep urine and droppings. This pervasive smell has been a reality for every pastoral and nomadic people throughout history: living with the warmth and smell of the animals that keep you alive. Just as I opened the fly sheet, and it flapped into the air, the same breeze lifted a meadow pipit and its partner into the sky for a burst of song. I took this as a good sign. The whole procedure was done with stealth and purpose, with what Roger Deakin called 'that instinctive blend of weariness and vigilance familiar to the unofficial camper.'[58] A landowner could appear at any moment to challenge me, but no one came.

As I trekked back to the car, the sun was dipping low in a chalky haze above Clare Island. This time, instead of following the sea's edge, I crossed the saltmarsh and headed for the machair. This briny ground with a dense fledge of sea pink is as near to flat and even as dry land can be, only a shout from the mudflats themselves. This evenness is what tempted developers in the late nineteenth century to buy out crofters in Scotland and manage the ground for links golf. Much western machair has been colonised by golfers ever since, though here at Murrevagh the golf course has taken only a small portion from the empire of grazing.

Moving from saltmarsh to machair, the sward hardened and was crossed with a fine geometry of sheep paths, orderly desire lines where the animals paced their routines. Small marks of history began to appear, the remains of white goalposts where someone thought of football before winds took away the ball and turned every game into a gale-blown chase beyond the touchlines. Then the most impressive relique of all: a standing stone marking the site of a children's burial ground or cillín, known here as garraí beag na bpáiste, the little garden of the children. The eight-foot orthostat is of red sandstone, probably from the local quarry on the Currane Peninsula, with a cluster of limestone rocks in a cordon around the base. These rocks, taken from the beach and rounded by wave action are deeply pitted, like sponges, and replace the white quartz of other ritual sites. Here limestone pays homage to sandstone, in the same relationship as obtains at the top of the second beach.

A plaque with the name in both languages fronts one side; a wrought-iron crucifix is attached to another. I choose one of the plain, unadorned faces for a photograph.

The Irish word garraí, garden, confers a quiet domestic innocence on the site; the sense of shelter and fruitfulness suggested by a garraí is denied by the exposed location, and the monument is not a place where I have ever lingered, pausing just briefly to pay my respects. Unbaptised or stillborn children were being consigned to limbo, a cold, neutral afterlife as heartless as the institutions set up in the nineteenth and twentieth centuries to concentrate social problems, including, most notoriously, the Mother and Baby Home at Tuam, Co. Galway. Research by Catherine

Corless, a local historian, has revealed that almost 800 babies were recorded as having died in the Bon Secours Home in Tuam, and concluded that most of these were buried in a mass grave near the building in disused underground sewage treatment chambers, though there is a suggestion that some death certs may have been falsified to allow for children to be adopted. The Tuam site, which is now the subject of extensive State-led research with the elaborate mechanisms of forensic science, is pitched somewhere between archaeology and crime-scene investigation. The scale of the inhumanity and neglect at Tuam has made thorough enquiry inevitable. At other sites, though, as here on the machair at Murrevagh, a different instinct prevails: one of quiet, respectful commemoration without the intrusion of excavations, DNA tests and radiocarbon dating. Even so, the sense of outrage and dismay at the scale of neglect and impunity at Tuam during the heyday of the Irish state in its Catholic identity, casts its shadow on smaller, less notorious sites such as this.

By the time I make my way across the last stretch of beach, colours have softened in the declining light: the sand has lost its tawny fire, and the rocks have a soft, chalky hue. The wind has also fallen, something I have often noticed at dusk: without a breeze, the thrum of waves is unchallenged. They are always there, the waves, coming and going: ag tuilleadh is ag trá a chaitheann an fharraige an lá.

Oystercatchers like a consignment of clockwork toys set loose on the machair poke rhythmically at the sward near the car: they fly briefly as I drive past, showing black-white wings like policemen.

As I went back to the village for some sustenance, I felt happy that I had my camp set up for the night and would not be leaving, but would return with the furnishing of my shelter: a mat, two sleeping bags, a head torch, and an extra layer of clothes should the night turn cold.

Two hours later I drove slowly back across the golf course under Orion. A man and his daughter and their dog walked past, the girl holding a torch. They saluted me without suspicion: bass anglers come here at night to fish the surf.

As it was still early evening, I sat in the car for some time. Mulranny was like a sequinned fortress overlooking the bay, raked by the beams of car headlights coming round the corner at the old railway hotel. The orange flames of a bonfire flared on the outskirts of the village, like a midsummer ritual, this one summoning the light. The Milky Way was a pale arch over Clew Bay, with one foot on Claggan Mountain. A zone of star-dissolving pallor hung on the southern horizon above Westport.

Eventually, there was a perceptible movement as the starry heaven shifted: just as the sun moves by day, the stars move at night following some pre-Copernican principle that still has a place in our perceptions.

While waiting, I had time to think about waiting, an experience that used to be commonplace for herders, sentries, fishermen, and others: their screen-free, radio-less waiting. Waiting where you count breaths, heartbeat, farts (so many per hour, as in Beckett's *Molloy*), or focus on small gestures: brushing teeth, manicuring nails, cleaning guns, repairing fishing gear.

The cultural fruits of waiting: the poems of the pastoral tradition were recited by young herders whiling away the time; the two boys in *Waiting for Godot* were employed by Godot to mind goats and sheep. Prayer and meditation as disciplines fostered by waiting.

We are very accustomed to TV images of waiting, as in the work of wildlife and adventure film-makers such as

Gordon Buchanan and Ben Fogle, but it all gets whittled down to brief summaries. We see short images of waiting, but we don't know waiting. Watching TV is not waiting. Seven hours in A&E is waiting: the outrage of waiting.

The night has clouded over, I have lost the stars. It is now a genuinely dark night, with no moon.

I will need my head torch to find the tent. The men who led Synge back through the sandhills on Inismaan at night did not have head torches.

The price of time: at a minimum hourly wage of €10, six minutes is one euro, or 3.6 seconds per cent.

I compose prayers while waiting:

For the child with its parents whom I saw on the beach earlier

For the girl with the lamp leading her father across the golf course in the dark

For all the little children who were buried under the machair at Murrevagh

For all the little babies whose remains were put in a septic tank at the Mother and Baby Home in Tuam

For a living future for all the children of this suffering planet.

Walking across the beach, without the headlight, the view ahead is a vague zonation of greys. Out on the sand, there's scarcely any sense of things shifting past, so you are held in the motion of walking itself. In order to find something to look at and focus on, I went to the water's edge where the foamy rim of waves appeared as white lines of fine fabric falling at my feet. On my way across the shingle, I disturbed several ringed plover, calling as they flew around me; and there was another, thinner, more ethereal, haunting call from a wader I did not recognise.

A bird flew up from the saltmarsh with a soft, whirring flutter and flickered briefly in the beam of my headlight: a woodcock?

I entered the field among the sheep's-eye reflections. One of them coughed a wheezy, sick-old-man cough. Several flies had got into the tent, among them some yellow-brown shit flies that I had to deal with. After much adjustment of sleeping bags and clothes, I managed to settle comfortably. The night was very mild for late February, and very quiet. There was no noise from the flax leaves. I slept.

At some stage towards morning, through my slumber I heard a skylark singing close by and thought of the story from Glendalough, where St Kevin is said to have banished the species following complaints from his workmen that they were being woken too early by the larks' song. But there was no other haunting: no circling screams and shrieks such as Macfarlane had heard as he lay in his bivouac at Chanctonbury Ring.

Eventually, I woke to the full light of morning. Then engine noise, as a vehicle approached across the machair and climbed the hillside near the tent. I wanted to introduce myself, to mutter a belated request for permission to camp, but by the time I had pulled on some clothes and stuck my head out of the tent, the Toyota Land Cruiser was on its way back down. The farmer had no interest in me. This amounted, in my mind, to a benevolence in keeping with the fairies of local tradition.

I stood up outside the tent in the brisk air of morning. The large mudflat was an exposed, busy street of birds and bird calls: curlews, uprooted from their homeland like a native people; noisy oystercatchers squabbling as ever; a flock of 134 barnacle geese; a scattering of *Tringa* waders: redshank and greenshank. A skylark struts around on top of one of the timber uprights, with a meadow pipit as a neighbour; they are enjoying this light, airy place with its early supply of insects.

A few solitary great northern divers are moving urgently across the bay on the other side, paddling strongly, patrolling the water for fish that must be moving in with the rising tide. They are close enough for me to see their strong brow and the vigorous swirl they leave in the water when they dive. A pale sun sits in the east above the silhouetted islands of Clew Bay – a calm, disciplined light with all the day ahead of it; this sun has none of the melancholy emotion of the evening.

As I am a nomad here, there's no time to linger: it is time to pack up and leave. As I do, and then move back down towards the gate, the air is busy with skylarks and pipits: they are already staking out their territories and, given favourable weather, will start to breed. It is remarkable how much of nature's business gets done early, even by May, and how many flowers are over before the holiday season. By the time the holidaymakers get to the beach, many flowers have gone to seed and most birds have fledged. By July, nature's summer cycle is winding down around the tourists and their enervation.

I'm called back to the beach by a beautiful, clean succession of waves: this is so much more appealing than crossing the desolate machair. With little wind, and some effect of atmospheric pressure further out, the calm bay is delivering orderly waves that break in a brilliant tuck of foam, and then subside, to become 'a million urgently typing fingers' rushing up the beach, which Tim Robinson described on Aran, at another muirbheach, Kilmurvey.[59] Some of the waves collapse in one simultaneous fold all across the line, but many also roll steadily from the side, making the tubes that surfers love, as the surf peels off cleanly.

I walk along the edge of surf, where the beery lines of the waves come to an end, and, as they wash up over my boots, and get dragged back, they make smaller waves, which collide with the larger incoming lines, at a slight angle. This produces a rapid ripping effect, as if a cable were being yanked violently off the surface, causing white water to spurt into the air.

A flock of forty sanderling is feeding at the waves' margin, picking tiny organisms from the backwash; they then take off in a tight bunch. Their world, as Elizabeth Bishop put it in her poem 'Sandpiper', 'is minute and vast and clear.' When they show their grey backs in flight, they are absorbed by the greys of the shore, but when they turn, showing their brilliant white underparts, the flock is transformed into a vibrant, white, moving tickertape, more urgent and compact than a starling murmuration. Bishop's poem presents these birds as curiously constrained by their feeding habits along the water's edge ('Poor bird, he is obsessed!') and ignores the jet-fighter, white-arrow speed and turns of flying sanderlings, with explosive energy picked from small grains of nourishment in the spilling wash.

By now it is nearly high tide, and I have to clamber across large rocks on the beachhead. Even without the encumbrance of camping gear, this is not something I normally do, electing to take a higher path, but this time there's a challenge in staggering across the top of the beach, balancing on rounded sandstone and limestone boulders, avoiding a few that are coated with slimy weed. When the waves withdraw, I can plash along the sand for a few paces before being driven back onto the rock by the next wave. I am adopting a strategy similar to the sanderling, living life at the edge, with the world being pulled from under me. Someone has built a section of dry-stone wall with flat slabs of red sandstone and a timber upright nearby as a kind of totem, a token of homage to Andy Goldsworthy. The symbolic impulse is here too, and I am not the first person to come here in search of meaning. My search for psychic presences here has proved fruitless; instead, I celebrate the secular glories of a fine morning by the breaking sea.

Afterword

One afternoon in the autumn of 2019, while this manuscript was in the final stages of revision, I set out to explore an area of low-lying blanket bog beside the sea on the west coast of Erris. The coast here is formed of creeks and shallow inlets reached by minor roads and tracks, a lonely, desolate place in most weathers. Heavy overnight rain had brought the rivers into spate, and there were new flashes of glitter on the bog from lying water. It was an airy, breezy sort of day, the threat of rain had passed, and tall stacks of cumulus were sliding across the horizon above Blacksod Bay.

I had with me an A4 detail from an OS map showing a minor road ending at a small group of houses; it looked as though there would be access from there to the shore just a couple of hundred metres away. I pulled in beside a brightly kept farmhouse and set out, going through a gate and passing an older cottage, which now served as an outhouse for storage. Having climbed over a second gateway at the end of the track, I was striding out across a stretch of poached ground when I heard a noise: distant, high-pitched. At first, I took it for a strange birdcall, but when I looked round, I saw a figure approaching from the top of a low ridge. This man was greatly agitated. I turned back to meet him and face a volley of outrage: *this is private land, you have no right to be here, who are you working for?*

I said calmly that I wasn't working for anyone but myself, that I was on my way to walk the shoreline, and that I kept some records of wildlife in the area. I had no business with farming, I assured him, to dispel any idea that I might be an inspector.

But why didn't you ask permission? Why didn't you call?

This, it turned out, was the nub of the issue: I had entered private land without asking permission, and the fault was mine.

This man's rage continued for a few moments.

People come onto land and get stuck there in the bog...

I agreed, people go into places they have no experience of; they drive big vehicles about the place; they leave gates unlocked.

Our conversation continued, and as I spoke with him about other farmers I had met in the area, and their concerns, we found common ground. The price of beef had slumped, the factories were not offering enough for farmers to earn a profit, and cattle farming in the west of Ireland was not viable. The last few times he was at the mart, he noticed that they were all older men; the young people would not stay in farming.

After that, he seemed reassured that I had no designs on his business; I could name some common acquaintances and was not a complete stranger; I even showed some native understanding of the plight of small farmers, having come from that stock on my mother's side. Eventually, although I had trespassed on his land, he muttered an apology for *rising up like that at you*, and we shook hands. I carried on, this time with his permission, and tried to reach the shore, but in the event had to turn back because the stream was in a high spate and I could not get across.

Such a confrontation, about access to land and rights of way, had often been mentioned in discussions about the landscape, but this was the first time I had met one full-on. I had proudly thought that my mild manner and general discretion would allow me to pass unchallenged, as they usually had in the past; but this time I had carelessly walked through another man's yard and not asked for permission to enter. On the strict matter of right, it was I who should have apologised, but the vehemence of his shouting at me had made me addled, and the violence of his manner left me dazed.

At the time of this altercation, there was a major confrontation between beef farmers and the meat processors about the price being paid to farmers for their carcasses. By early September, most meat plants in the country had been shut down by a blockade of farmers despairing at the paltry prices being paid. At the same time, the situation was particularly acute because Chinese inspectors were visiting, and the trade with China was seen as a vital part of the beef industry, in view of falling consumption in Europe. Exports to China had started some months earlier, after years of negotiation to satisfy Chinese officials, and this valuable link was now being put at risk.

The man I met had a few cattle grazing along the boggy margins of the stream I had failed to cross. We had agreed that the many bright new homes being built in north Mayo were not being paid for by such farming: it was money from England, from the building trade in London and Birmingham, which paid for those houses, many of them second homes that would be vacant for much of the year.

As well as the history of emigration from Mayo, I felt that in our conversation we even had global trade and politics weighing on our concerns. China's authoritarian government was involved in a major standoff with protestors in Hong Kong, who had brought the state to a standstill, demanding that the Governor Carrie Lam's extradition bill be withdrawn, as it eventually was. The blockade of the Irish meat factories, I felt, was another act of defiance of China's authority: the despair of the beef farmers reflected globalisation, large-scale production and the oppression of the peasantry world-wide.

My carelessness that day came from the thought that I was going to a *wild*, remote place where I would be leaving common obligations behind. This is a mistake that has often been made by visitors, who underestimate the intensity of territories and divisions. The same mistake was made by Shell, in the initial stages of its development of the Corrib gas field off the coast of north Mayo: promoters of the project thought that they could ride roughshod over the views of local people; in the event, they paid a heavy price and provoked a backlash that still hangs in the air to this day.

I have kept the sheet with the map detail for the area I had not been able to reach. A large stretch of forestry marked in the east does not exist: the area must have been in state forestry plans imported into the map by the Ordnance Survey, but it was never planted. The main thing missing, though, is a symbol or device to mark a farmer's anger, something like the sea creatures drawn on early modern maps to denote the unpredictable, and the limits of knowledge. Perhaps a drawing of a large man with windblown hair waving a heavy stick.

Where all this leaves ideas of the wild and wilderness is a moot point. Some people are completely dismissive of the notion that there is wilderness anywhere in Ireland, given the intensity of conflict over land: even on remote mountaintops the ground is marked by old and new boundary lines, and signs of grazing livestock are everywhere.

My run-in with that farmer was another instance of a visitor with naïve expectations coming up against reality on the ground, part of a pattern so old that it went beyond cliché. I had wanted to reach a wild place and instead had been checked by a victim of globalised society, shouting in my face with suspicion of officialdom, anxieties about legal liability, and anger at the greed of big industry. You find this trend repeated in the softer atmosphere of culture. Lady Morgan's hero came to the west of Ireland with romantic expectations of native purity, only to discover that his wild Irish girl was reading current periodical literature from London. Synge's Aran islanders were eager for news of foreign wars. Again and again, the excursionist's fantasy of escape from culture, into the wild, into innocence, is flatly contradicted by experience.

The proponents of the Wild Nephin project are probably right when they advertise the possibility of primitive recreation as the core attraction of the area. There is little mention in their consultation documents of local people and their traditions, or of cultural remains in the landscape. The experience is presented as a solitary one, an apprehension of wilderness beyond language. However, in my wanderings in north Mayo and elsewhere, the experience of wilderness has usually harboured the possibility of being disrupted or even subverted by some element of human witness, some new knowledge that can transform the place, not out of wildness, but into a deeper sense of what it is to endure at the edge of things.[60]

Glossary

The following list gives common placename terms referred to in the book, most of which derive from Irish. Although Irish is now extinct as a vernacular in the Wild Nephin area, many topographical terms are preserved in current placenames, usually in anglicised versions. These are given in parentheses.

abhainn (owen)   river

ailp (alp)   lump; knob

ailt (allt)   steep-sided glen; river gorge

bábhún (bawn)   walled enclosure; sheepfold

binn (ben)   mountain peak; brow of cliff, etc.

buaile (booley)   summer pasture and/or the associated huts and enclosures

bun   lower end or base of mountain, river etc.

carrach   rocky, rough

cloigeann (claggan)   head

coire (corrie)   steep-sided hollow under a hill or mountain formed by glacial action, often containing a lake

comhra(i)c (corick)   confluence of rivers or streams

cruach (croagh)   mountain peak or hilltop; 'a symmetrically shaped mountain' (Dineen). Also **cruachán** (croaghaun)

díogan (deegan)   trench; narrow, steep-sided valley

doire (derry)   (oak) wood

droim (drum)   back; ridge

dubh (duff, doo)   black, dark: refers to an area with prevailing shadow from overlooking heights, or to water bodies with dark banks of peat

éadan   brow of ridge or hillside

eiscir (esker)   ridge formed by glacial deposition

erris, see **iorras**

fiodán (fiddaun)   small stream, often the first appearance of flowing water at the edge of catchments

flow country   Atlantic blanket bog characterised by small lakes or bog pools (locháns), a term first coined by the Scottish conservationist Derek Ratcliffe

gabhlán (gaulaun)   fork; junction

garbh (garve)   rough, rocky

gorm   blue; the lustre of bare rock on a mountainside

iorras (erris)   peninsula, headland

leitir (letter)   hillside

levee	protective bank forming a boundary to prevent flooding and incursion by livestock
lochán	small bog lake or pool
mám (maum)	upland pass
mearing	boundary
moing (mong)	mossy swamp or fen
molinia	purple moor grass, *Molinia caerulea*: a characteristic plant in the area, especially at lower altitudes, forming dense tussocks
muirbheach (murrevagh)	
	machair: sandy flatland near the sea
néifinn (nephin)	sacred place or grove; little chapel
nioscóid	eminence or swelling on an upland ridge
ogúl (uggool)	hollow place (Fiachra MacGabhann)
owen, see **abhainn**	
poll	hollow place; hole
raithneach (ranny)	fern, bracken
redd	area of loose gravel in the bed of a river where salmon spawn
scairdeán (scardaun)	cascade
scailp	rocky fissure; cave
screig	rocky crag

seanchaí (shanachie) plural **seanchaithe**
storyteller

sheugh sluggish stream or drain

sián (sheean) fairy mound

sraith (srah) level stretch of ground near a river formed by deposition of sediments, affording valuable areas of pasture in the bog

talus terrain with large boulders formed by cliff fall

tairseachán (tarsaghaun)
threshold; boundary to another territory

tamhnach (tawny) upland field or pasture

torc 1.wild boar 2.summit

ucht chest, breast of ridge, hill etc.

Acknowledgements

I am indebted to the people who shared their knowledge, gave me their time, or took me under their wing during my explorations in Wild Nephin. I'd like to record special thanks to: Jean Beattie, John Booth, Patrick Carey, Michael Chambers, Moirín Chambers, Susan Callaghan, Pat Coughlan, Barry Dalby, Derek Davidson, Eleanor de Eyto, Tom Dempsey, Ged Dowling, Margaret Flaherty, Guy and Sibylle Geffroy, Mark Granier, Adrian Hendroff, Lynda Huxley, Michael Kingdon, Liam Lysaght, Paud McHugh and his late father Paddy McHugh, Frank McManamon, Georgia MacMillan, Liamy Mac Nally, Derek McLoughlin, Jean-Pierre and William Maire, Kevin Martin, Fintan Masterson, Anthony Mayock, Alan Mee, Marina Mulligan, Barry Murphy, Ciara Ní Mhurchú, John O'Callaghan, Michael O'Connell, Jim O'Connor, Fergal O'Dowd, Nicola Stronach, Ramona Usher.

I can't include an unnamed couple who served me tea and apple tart after a walk near Belderg years ago because we never introduced each other; while their farm near Benmore is outside the Wild Nephin area, their generosity exemplifies for me the spirit of North Mayo.

Patricia Kuester, Chris Huxley and my wife Jessica read the draft manuscript and made many valuable suggestions for revision. Yvonne McDermott has again come up with a fine map of local detail for Tarsaghaunmore, where my fascination started, and Éadaoin Ní Néill of Aperture Web Design compiled the area map. Maria McDermott gave crucial technical help at a late stage and Ursula Peters revisited memories of our walk at Srahduggaun several years ago to design the beautiful cover.

My poem 'Snow Bunting' from *The Clare Island Survey* (1991) is reprinted with permission from Gallery Press.

NOTES

[1] Mícheál Mac Énrí, 'Seanchas ó Iorrus', *Béaloideas*, 13, 1943, pp. 173-237 (p. 173).

[2] Séamas Ó Catháin, 'Folklore Collecting in Mayo under the Auspices of the Irish Folklore Commission (1935-1970), in *Mayo: History and Society*, edited by Gerard Moran and Nollaig Ó Muraíle (Dublin: Geography Publications, 2014), pp. 635-47.

[3] Paul Evans, *Field Notes from the Edge: Journeys through Britain's Secret Wilderness* (London: Rider Books, 2015), p. x.

[4] Micheál Ó Gallchobhair, 'Amhráin Ó Iorrus', *Béaloideas*, 10, 1940, pp. 210-84 (252-55).

[5] Pádraig Ó Moghráin, 'Corrigenda and Notes to "Amhráin Ó Iorrus"', *Béaloideas*, 13, 1943, pp. 292-94.

[6] Dan O'Brien, *The Rites of Autumn* (London: Collins, 1988), p. 30.

[7] J.A. Baker, *The Peregrine* (1967; New York: New York Review, 2005), p. 41.

[8] Helen Macdonald, *H is for Hawk* (London: Jonathan Cape, 2014), p. 79.

[9] Macdonald, *H is for Hawk*, p. 86.

[10] Patrick Mullarkey, *Ballycroy and Beyond* (Private publication, 2014), pp. 74-77.

[11] Sir Ralph Payne-Gallwey, *The Fowler in Ireland* (London: Van Voorst, 1882), pp. 228-29.

[12] Payne-Gallwey, *The Fowler*, pp. 226-27

[13] Graham Appleton, 'Snipe and Jack Snipe in the UK and Ireland', wadertales.wordpress.com.

[14] Gerald Fitzgerald, *Pot Luck: Rough Shooting in the West of Ireland* (London: Herbert Jenkins, 1938), p. 47.

[15] Simon Schama, *Landscape and Memory* (London: HarperCollins, 1995), p. 463.

[16] Robert Macfarlane, *Mountains of the Mind: A History of a Fascination* (London: Granta, 2003), pp. 112-17.

[17] John McVeagh, *Richard Pococke's Irish Tours* (Dublin: Irish Academic Press, 1995), p. 80.

[18] See, for example, John Bush, *Hibernia Curiosa: A Letter from a Gentleman in Dublin to his Friend at Dover in Kent* (London: Flexney, 1769).

[19] Bush, *Hibernia Curiosa*, p. 41.

[20] McVeagh, *Pococke's Irish Tours*, p. 81.

[21] Robert Macfarlane, *The Wild Places* (London: Granta, 2007), p.78.

[22] Derek Mahon, *Antarctica* (Loughcrew: Gallery Press, 1985).

[23] Seamas Caulfield, 'Céide Fields and Belderrig Valley: Four Score Years of Research', in *Mayo: History and Society*, edited by Gerard Moran and Nollaig Ó Muraíle (Dublin: Geography Publications, 2014), pp. 25-44; Peter Coxon, *A Field Guide to the Quaternary of North Mayo* (Dublin: Irish Association for Quaternary Studies, 1991).

[24] Michael O'Connell and Karen Molloy, 'Farming and Woodland Dynamics in Ireland during the Neolithic', *Biology and Environment: Proceedings of the Royal Irish Academy*, Volume 101B, No. 1-2, pp. 99-128, (p.116); Bernard O'Hara, 'An Introduction to Archaeological Monuments in County Mayo', in *Mayo: History and Society*, edited by Gerard Moran and Nollaig Ó Muraíle (Dublin: Geography Publications, 2014), pp. 1-24.

[25] Robert Macfarlane, *Underland: A Deep Time Journey* (London: Hamish Hamilton, 2019), p. 26.

[26] Tim Robinson, *Connemara: The Last Pool of Darkness* (Dublin: Penguin Ireland, 2008), p. 133; Evans, *Field Notes from the Edge*, p. 188.

[27] John F. Deane, *The Works of Love: Incarnation, Ecology and Poetry* (Dublin: Columba Press, 2010), pp. 326-31.

[28] Desmond and Maimie Nethersole-Thompson, *Greenshanks* (Berkhamstead: Poyser, 1979), p. 42.

[29] Nethersole-Thompson, *Greenshanks*, p. 34.

[30] Nethersole-Thompson, *Greenshanks*, pp. 112-13.

[31] Elma Brazel, 'The Physical Landscape of Treanlaur', *Connaught Telegraph*, 4th August 2004.

[32] Pádraig Ó Móráin's 1949 article in *Béaloideas*, 'Gearr-Chuntas ar an Athair Mánus Mac Suibhne', XVII, is translated and edited by Sheila Mulloy in *Father Manus Sweeney, a Mayo Priest in the Rebellion of 1798* (Westport: Westport Historical Society, 1999).

[33] Horatio Clare, 'To the far side of the edge,' *Financial Times*, 24/25 November 2018.

[34] Trevor Fisher, Facebook in litt, 20.9.2019.

[35] Pauline Barrett, *The Addergoole Titanic Story* (Lahardaun: Addergoole Titanic Society, 2010); Nick Barratt, *Lost Voices from the Titanic* (London: Preface Publishing, 2009).

[36] Jim Crumley, *The Nature of Winter* (Salford: Saraband, 2017), p. 11.

[37] Schama, *Landscape and Memory*, pp.185-201.

[38] National Parks and Wildlife Service, *Wild Nephin Wilderness Area: Conversion Plan (2018-2033)* (Dublin: SLR Consulting, 2018), Executive Summary, p. 6.

[39] Robert Lloyd Praeger, *The Way that I Went: An Irishman in Ireland* (Dublin: Allen Figgis, 1937), p. 206.

[40] Jeremy Mill, 'Two Kinds of Wilderness', *Orion*, March/April 2017, 34-43, p. 41.

[41] 'Two Kinds of Wilderness', p. 42.

[42] Séamas Ó Catháin, 'Folklore Collecting in Mayo under the Auspices of the Irish Folklore Commission (1935-1970),' in *Mayo: History and Society* (Dublin: Geography Publications, 2014), pp. 635-47.

[43] Amhlaoibh Ó Súileabháin, *Cinnlae: The Diary of Humphrey O'Sullivan*, edited by Michael McGrath, four volumes (London: Irish Texts Society, 1928-1931), volume I, pp. 295 and 325.

[44] *Cinnlae*, volume II, p. 21.

[45] *Cinnlae*, volume IV, p. 256.

[46] *Cinnlae*, volume IV, pp. 117-19.

[47] *Cinnlae*, volume IV, p. 135.

[48] *Cinnlae*, volume IV, pp. 255-57.

[49] *Cinnlae*, volume IV, p. 283.

[50] Antonia McManus, *The Irish Hedge School and Its Books 1695-1831* (Dublin: Four Courts Press, 2002), p. 185.

[51] McManus, *Irish Hedge School*, p. 215.

[52] Sydney Owenson, Lady Morgan, *The Wild Irish Girl* (1806; Oxford: Oxford University Press, 1999), p. 157.

[53] *Cinnlae*, volume IV, p. 129.

[54] *Cinnlae*, volume IV, p. 215.

[55] *A Short Account of the History of Burrishoole Parish*, edited by Liamy MacNally (1957; Westport: Covie Publications and Recordings, 2004), p. 6.

[56] Robert Macfarlane, *The Old Ways* (London: Hamish Hamilton, 2012), pp. 316-19.

[57] Nan Shepherd, *The Living Mountain* (1977; Edinburgh: Canongate, 2011), p. 90.

[58] Roger Deakin, *Wildwood: A Journey through Trees* (London: Hamish Hamilton, 2007), p. 85.

[59] Tim Robinson, *Stones of Aran: Pilgrimage* (Dublin: Lilliput Press, 1986), p. 176.

INDEX

INDEX

INDEX

INDEX

Nordmann's Greenshank